The Fickle Finger
of Lady Death
and Other Plays

Taft Memorial Fund
and University of Cincinnati
Studies in Latin American, Chicano,
and U.S. Latino Theatre

Kirsten F. Nigro
General Editor

Vol. 5

PETER LANG
New York • Washington, D.C./Baltimore
Bern • Frankfurt am Main • Berlin • Vienna • Paris

The Fickle Finger of Lady Death and Other Plays

Translated by

Carlos Morton

PETER LANG
New York • Washington, D.C./Baltimore
Bern • Frankfurt am Main • Berlin • Vienna • Paris

Library of Congress Cataloging-in-Publication Data

The fickle finger of Lady Death and other plays/
[translated by] Carlos Morton.
p.   cm. — (Taft Memorial Fund and University of Cincinnati studies
in Latin American, Chicano, and U.S. Latino theatre; vol. 5)
Includes bibliographical references.
Contents: The Tree / [Elena Garro]—Profane games / [Carlos Olmos]—
Fickle finger of Lady Death / [Eduardo Rodríguez Solís]—Murder with
malice / [Víctor Hugo Rascón Banda].
1. Mexican drama—20th century—Translations into English. I. Morton,
Carlos. II. Series: Taft Memorial Fund and University of Cincinnati studies in
Latin American, Chicano, and U.S. Latino theatre; v. 5.
PQ7271.E5F6   862—dc20   94-37489
ISBN 0-8204-2525-7
ISSN 1062-5453

Die Deutsche Bibliothek-CIP-Einheitsaufnahme

The fickle finger of Lady Death and other plays/transl. by Carlos Morton. -
New York; Washington, D.C./Baltimore; Bern; Frankfurt am Main;
Berlin; Vienna; Paris: Lang.
(Taft Memorial Fund and University of Cincinnati studies in Latin American,
Chicano, and U.S. Latino theatre; Vol. 5)
ISBN 0-8204-2525-7
NE: Morton, Carlos [Übers.]; GT

TABLE OF CONTENTS

Illustrations

TABLE OF ILLUSTRATIONS

Illustrations

INTRODUCTION

Mexican drama in the latter part of the twentieth century has been characterized by a wide range of styles, representing a departure and an escape from the strict realism that dominated in the 1950s and 1960s. Four of those styles are represented in this collection of translations by Carlos Morton. The range includes the kind of magic realism that underlies the situation and the relation between the two female characters in Elena Garro's *The Tree* with its aura of death that, little by little, casts its shadow over Marta. The absurdist *Profane Games*, by Carlos Olmos, presents the perverted relations between a sister, a brother and their (dead?) parents, a relationship that has enclosed them in a house where existence revolves around games between the living and the dead. Eduardo Rodríguez Solís's *The Fickle Finger of Lady Death* shows different guises of death in a kind of dance hall atmosphere that mixes humor and violence. Finally Víctor Hugo Rascón Banda's documentary play, *Murder with Malice*, depicts the circumstances surrounding the death of a Chicano boy at the hands of the Dallas, Texas police. Together the four plays serve as examples of the wide variety of styles that characterize contemporary Mexican theater.

Although the plays represent different styles, they have at least two elements in common. One is the period in which they were written, between the late 1960s (*The Tree*, 1967) and the early 1990s (*Murder with Malice*, 1993), a period in which Mexican plays and playwrights were struggling to regain respectability and looking for new ways to communicate their ideas and their concerns. Thus, while the four playwrights represented here come from different backgrounds and different experiences, the plays do share a common genesis: the period of the *Nueva Dramaturgia* (New Drama), the years of the struggle to make Mexican drama acceptable again.

The second shared element is the presence of death as a driving force of life. This reflects the attraction of death in Mexican culture, described by Octavio Paz in the *The Labyrinth of Solitude*. It is no coincidence that Paz discusses the Mexican concept of death in the same chapter where he talks about parties ("*The Day of the Dead*"). The Mexican "indifference" to and "contempt" for death make it easy to include it in their "fiestas..., games..., loves and...thoughts." This is nowhere more clear than in *Profane Games*, in which a game grows out of death and vice-versa, and in *The Fickle Finger of Lady Death*, a playful contemplation of death. Death is also the step that initiates the action of *Murder with Malice*, and it is the step that awaits in *The Tree*. That presence constitutes its significance here: it is the common thread that runs through all four plays included in this collection. There are, however, additional elements that bind them.

Although Elena Garro (1922) and Carlos Olmos (1947) come from different generations, *The Tree* (1967) and *Profane Games* (1970) are strikingly similar. Both revolve around the themes of death and guilt, both have to do with uncertain and uncommon relationships, both contain a thread of black humor, and both require the audience to work out mysteries concerning past deaths and current threats while at the same time trying to make some sense of the characters. Both have elements of absurdist theater running through the dialogue, the situations and the characters. Although neither play treats the problems created by the generation gap in the form most commonly portrayed at the time in Mexico (the late 1960s and early 1970s), the actions do grow out of flawed family relationships. Garro's play is the more lyrical and mysterious of the two, while Olmos's is the more winding and treacherous. Both works anticipate the themes of unstable or created realities that would become so prevalent ten years later.

Elena Garro's *The Tree* is one of a number of short plays by her that, to some extent, share the flavor of some of the works by one of her most important contemporaries, Emilio Carballido. *The Tree* leads the viewer in several directions. It features a lyric element, almost dream-like, such as that in plays by Oscar Villegas, Jesús González Dávila and Gerardo Velásquez, who belong to a more recent generation, but who were also writing as the 1970s began. *The Tree*, at least in the beginning, recalls the Chilean Egon *Wolff's Flores de Papel (Paper Flowers)*, with its mysterious character who comes into a lonely woman's home and slowly takes control of her personality. In Garros's play the mystery and the resulting fear brought by Luisa give her a power over Marta that could become total, depending on one's interpretation of the play's title object. The fact that Luisa could literally communicate with a tree brings a touch of magic realism; if the image inherent in that communication reflects Luisa's contact with Marta, a darker magic emerges and threatens to overwhelm and eventually doom Marta.

The characters in Olmos's *Profane Games* are already doomed. The Oedipal, Electra and incestuous relationships that slowly reveal themselves condemn Saul and Alma to a kind of emotional prison. The murder of their parents tightens the chains, and the suggestion at the end that Saul and Alma might in fact be the parents, who murdered their children to end the incest and the jealousy, is the final link that guarantees that the two characters will be locked together forever. The play, whose role playing characters sometimes speak for themselves and sometimes for others, is much more sophisticated than most of the parents-versus-children works that were so common around the time the play was written and, naturally, it presents a bigger challenge to an audience than the psychological realism that was used so commonly to comment on the generation gap.

The Fickle Finger of Lady Death, by Eduardo Rodríguez Solís, is the most "Mexican" of the four works, but it is universal in its satire of contemporary society's new deadly sins: gluttony, jealousy, lust, drunkenness, nosiness, obsessive weight loss and the addiction to television. Amid non-stop word play and jokes, the seven short scenes, overseen by Death herself, follow the characters to their ultimate demise. This is one of the plays that turned away from the more common generation gap theme and focused instead on aspects of Mexican culture and society. It also left behind the current of long-suffering plays and used humor as a way of expressing its ideas and its criticism.

The inherent condemnation in *Murder with Malice*, by Rascón Banda, continues the vein of social criticism that runs through virtually all of his plays, no matter what the form. His drama shows as much variety as any contemporary Mexican playwright; he has written everything from poetic works (*Voces en el umbral*) (*Voices at the Door*), to plays based on historical figures (*Tina Moddotti*), to almost mythical plays about wrestling (*Máscara vs. Cabellera*), to realistic, and even documentary plays. *Murder with Malice* falls into this latter category. This time the action takes place north of the border, in Dallas, and relates a real-life incident that still echoes through the Chicano community. The play portrays the circumstances surrounding the killing of a twelve-year old Chicano boy by a Dallas police officer. The action, which includes sections taken directly from trial transcripts, reveals the racism that drove the events. It tackles not only the specific incident, but the overriding question of justice. In common with the other three plays included here is the presence of death as a driving force of life.

Since the mid-1980s Mexican theater, on the basis of a growing number of quality dramas, has slowly fought its way back from near death to a new life. Works by playwrights like Sabina Berman, Víctor Hugo Rascón Banda and Jesús González Dávila join plays by Carballido and Vicente Leñero in theaters on a regular basis. At the same time that they have begun to be accepted by the Mexican theater-going public, the excellence of their works is also attracting attention abroad. Carballido has for years been a staple at Hispanic theater conferences in the United States, and recently Berman has been appearing as frequently. Little by little the plays are making their way to U.S. stages. Three of the plays in this collection, for example, have been produced in translation in Texas, by Teatro Dallas, and there are numerous theater companies and foundations regularly staging Mexican plays from New York to Los Angeles. *The Fickle Finger of Lady Death* was staged by an equity cast during August of 1994 by the Puerto Rican Traveling Theater in New York City. Of course they stage works in Spanish, but more and more bilingual works and works in translation have been made available to the public. The obvious obstacle to even more plays making their way north of the border is the hurdle imposed by language. Collections like this one by Carlos Morton, though, help to transcend that barrier. His translations faithfully reproduce the lyricism, the humor and the tension present in the Spanish-language versions and help a reader or spectator to experience the true flavor of the original texts. With more access to plays, the English-speaking public will be able to discover what Mexican audiences are discovering every day: Mexican playwrights have important ideas to communicate, and they are communicating them in ways that are both enlightening and entertaining. The more translations we have, such as those in this volume, the sooner we will all be able to benefit from their work.

Ronald D. Burgess
Gettysburg College

NOTE FROM THE TRANSLATOR

Although the works of contemporary Mexican playwrights are becoming better known in the United States, good translations for the stage are not readily available. Too often the renderings are more "academic" than performance oriented and thus lack a distinctive dramatic style. In truth, it takes a playwright to translate a playwright. In consultation with the authors, I have taken poetic license with the versions in this anthology of contemporary Mexican drama. Rather than a literary exercise; they are meant to be produced.

I didn't start out to be a translator. I began at the urging of Cora Cardona, artistic director of Teatro Dallas, while I was on a Fulbright at the National University of Mexico in 1989-90. Ms. Cardona, a graduate of the prestigious *Instituto Nacional de Bellas Artes* in Mexico, wanted to stage numerous contemporary Mexican plays in Dallas, Texas but expressed frustration at the inadequate and often literal translations available. Cora had produced my *Johnny Tenorio* several times, and commissioned me to write *The Fatherless*, a play about Hispanic gangs set in El Paso, Texas. She expressed confidence that a Chicano playwright like myself, who is English dominant but proficient in Spanish, would be a natural translator.

The first play I was commissioned to translate was Carlos Olmos's *Juegos Profanos (Profane Games)*, part of a trilogy he began in 1970. Since I was in Mexico City at the time, I was able to work very closely with the playwright, who read the translation and gave me notes. The English language version of this play was produced by Teatro Dallas and further developed during a staged reading at the University of California, Riverside in 1991.

Pleased by the translation I did of Olmos play, Cardona commissioned me to translate *El árbol (The Tree)* by the well known writer Elena Garro. The English-language version was produced by Teatro Dallas in 1993 and given a staged reading at the University of California, Riverside the same year.

The third play I translated for Teatro Dallas was *Santos,* by Víctor Hugo Rascón Banda, which deals with the murder of a twelve-year old Chicano boy at the hands of a Dallas police officer. *Santos* had its premier July 1993 at Teatro Dallas. The author then composed a new version of the play entitled *Homicidio Calificado (Murder with Malice)*, which was produced in Mexico City in 1994, and which is included in this anthology.

The fourth play in the collection is by Eduardo Rodríguez Solís, *Las ondas de la Catrina (The Fickle Finger of Lady Death)*. Rodríguez Solís had translated my *Johnny Tenorio* into Spanish in 1989 and then secured funding for a production sponsored by the National Autonomous University of Mexico and the Programa Cultural de Las Fronteras. The play premiered at the Festival Cervantino and ran for approximately one month in downtown Mexico City. I returned the favor by translating one of Rodríguez Solís's plays. In 1993 *The Fickle Finger of Lady Death* had a staged reading during the New Plays Festival at the University of California, Riverside under the direction of Jorge Huerta. Huerta was so impressed by the play and the positive audience reaction that he proposed it to the producer of the Puerto Rican Traveling Theater, Miriam Colón. The original Spanish version and the English translation were performed in the summer of 1994 in New York City as part of an equity production directed by Jorge Huerta.

Besides all of the above people and institutions, this book could not have been possible without the guidance and proofreading of Kirsten F. Nigro, editor of the *Taft Memorial Fund and University of Cincinnati Studies in Latin American, Chicano and U.S. Latino Theater.* I must also thank Dora A. Velasco for inputing the book into the computer and getting it camera ready. Funding sources for the completion of the manuscript included the UCR-Mexico Collaborative Research and Training Group at UC Riverside for a modest Travel Grant to collaborate with the authors. I especially want to thank the University of California Institute for Mexico and the United States (UC MEXUS) and its director, Juan-Vicente Palerm, for the additional funding to publish this anthology.

Carlos Morton
University of California, Riverside

THE TREE

by

ELENA GARRO

TRANSLATED FROM THE SPANISH

by

CARLOS MORTON

The English-language premier of THE TREE took place on March 3, 1993 in Dallas, Texas. It was produced by Teatro Dallas and directed by Eduardo Ruiz Savinon.

CHARACTERS

MARTA, *Fifty years old*
LUISA, *Fifty-seven years old*

THE SCENE

Present-day Mexico City

(Interior of Marta's house in Mexico City. A large and spacious suite, furnished with elegant antiques. The floors are carpeted, and on the high ceilings hang mirrors and paintings. The curtains are shut. A great silence reigns. Marta, seated in a chaise longue, is reading. The front doorbell rings violently, resounding through the house. Marta is startled. The doorbell rings again, even more violently. Marta rises.)

MARTA. Who could it be? *(She exits. The doorbell continues ringing with increased intensity. All at once it stops. After a few beats Marta enters the house followed by Luisa, who barges in behind her and collapses on the sofa. She is dirty and her clothes are torn. Marta looks at her, half disinterested, half curious, as though she knew her from many years past.)* What brings you to Mexico City?...What happened, Luisa? *(Luisa straightens up with a start. She lifts up her soiled skirts and points to a black and blue mark on her stomach. Then she points to a bruise on her nose. Then her ear, from which runs a sliver of partly coagulated blood.)*

LUISA. Julian!

MARTA. Julian?

LUISA. Yes, Julian beat me.

MARTA. That's not true, Luisa. Tell me the truth. *(Beat.)* Tell me! Tell me what happened. Do you know what they say in the village? A good man usually ends up with a bitch of a wife. And you, Luisa, hound your husband like a bitch.

LUISA. Me, a bitch, Martita?

MARTA. Yes, like a bitch. And you're driving him crazy.

LUISA. Crazy, Martita? He always hits me, always! Always!

MARTA. For God's sake, Luisa, don't say bad things about him! Remember that Julian worked in my father's house and I've known him since I was a child. On the other hand, when I met you I thought you were a very infantile woman...

LUISA. *(Interrupting her with laughter.)* Infantile, Martita?

MARTA. Don't laugh...your laughter makes me nervous. *(Marta stares at the Indian woman who keeps laughing, covering her mouth with her hand. After a time she calms down.)*

LUISA. Julian is bad, Martita, very bad!

MARTA. Shut up! Don't say any more stupid things. If he's so bad, why is he so well respected? Why does everyone seek his advice?

LUISA. He makes me cry! He makes me cry!

MARTA. *(Impatiently.)* He makes you cry! My God, Luisa, you're too touchy. Do you know what I think, if Julian beats you it's because you deserve it.

LUISA. No, Martita, I don't deserve it! Julian is bad, very bad. *(Luisa rises from the sofa and suddenly throws herself on top of Marta, covering her with kisses. Marta allows herself to be kissed, trying to hide the disgust she holds for the Indian woman. Luisa suddenly gets up and falls down on the couch again. She wipes her tears away with dirty fingers. Marta observes her with disdain.)*

MARTA. Just look at you! The picture of misery! But I don't feel sorry for you. It's your fault. You're too stubborn! How many times have I scolded you? How many times have I told you to change your ways? I'm tired of dealing with you. You don't listen to anyone and only think of yourself. I'm sick and tired of you, I really am.

LUISA. What about him? He always beats me, always. He's evil, Martita, evil!

MARTA. *(Wringing her hands.)* I have to be patient with you, Luisa. Oh God, my God! How could you let one of your creatures turn out like this?

LUISA. Which way, Martita, which way?

MARTA. Nothing, Luisa...now tell me, what is it you want? You can't sit there all afternoon. I'll fix you something to eat.

LUISA. No, no, Martita, don't bother!

MARTA. What do you mean, don't bother? You must be dying of hunger.

LUISA. Yes, yes, Martita, I haven't eaten all day...but don't bother, let your servants do it...

MARTA. The girls aren't here. It's their day off. They're not coming back until bright and early tomorrow morning.

LUISA. Tomorrow morning? Then, don't bother.

MARTA. You're crazy! I'm going to get you a bite to eat. *(Marta exits. Luisa looks around in a daze at all the furnishings. After a time she cleans her ear, then stares at the blood on her finger. She waits with a sigh of resignation. Enter Marta. She has a bundle of old clothes. Luisa gets up with a start and approaches Marta, who backs off visibly repulsed by the Indian woman's filthiness.)*

LUISA. Martita...*(Marta doesn't answer her. Luisa starts to cry.)* Martita...just leave my children out of this. It's true that they don't need me anymore. They've grown up.

MARTA. Don't cry, Luisa...

LUISA. Leave my children out of this...

MARTA. You've never cared about your children. They were barely born when you went out on the street, running after Julian. They survived, thanks to the care given to them by the neighbors. Poor children! Always crying: "Mama, let Papa go. Stay home..." And now you tell me you're crying for them?

LUISA. Yes, Martita, I'm crying for them.

MARTA. Well, don't cry, because your tears don't move me. I want to know why you bother Julian night and day...

LUISA. That's the way he wants it, Martita, he doesn't like to be alone...*(Luisa smiles stupidly.)*

MARTA. Good God in Heaven! The poor man complains that you don't even let him go to the bathroom.

LUISA. *(Calmly.)* Things aren't the same here as they are over there. There we do it in the ditch...

MARTA. *(Angry.)* What are you saying! You do it in the ditch! Do you think I'm so stupid as to believe something like that?

LUISA. *(Smiling.)* No, Martita, over there we do it in the ditch. *(Luisa gazes calmly at Marta who angrily throws the bundle of old clothes down on an armchair.)*

MARTA. Don't make me angry, Luisa.

LUISA. Martita, over there we do it in the ditch and it's very dark, Martita, very dark. *(Marta doesn't answer and Luisa curls up on the couch and starts to cry.)*

MARTA. Don't cry...what are you doing now?

LUISA. It's very dark, Martita...here there's a lot of light, but there it's dark, all black and ugly Martita, very ugly.

MARTA. I know it, Luisa. Now, cheer up, there's plenty of light here. You can stay a few days with me if you like. Where will you go? No one wants you.

LUISA. That's true, Martita, no one wants me.

MARTA. No one wants you because you're bad. If you behave yourself I'll take you to the movies. Have you ever been to the movies?

LUISA. *(Getting up abruptly and approaching Marta.)* To the movies? No, Martita, no.

MARTA. *(Pulling away from the Indian woman.)* Well, one of these days I'll take you...now you have to eat something. You look like you're dying of hunger...and when you finish eating you will take a bath.

LUISA. *(Coming closer.)* Where, Martita, where?

MARTA. Where what?

LUISA. Where do I take a bath?

MARTA. Calm down, Luisa! There's no hurry, eat first, then take a bath and change your clothes. *(Grabbing the bundle of clothes.)*

LUISA. *(Interrupting.)* Thank you, Martita, thank you! May God bless you. I brought my own clothes. Before I left my house I took them with me and left, all alone...I didn't have any place to go. I was walking, walking, and all at once I saw Martita's face before me and I said to myself: I'm going with her. She's such a good person...*(Luisa unravels her rebozo, takes out her old, faded clothes, and shows them to Marta. Marta, embarrassed, doesn't know what to do with the clothes.)*

LUISA. That's how I got here, with Martita's face in front of me, guiding my way.

MARTA. Oh, Luisa! I'm going to get you some coffee...

LUISA. No, Martita! I better take a bath, that way you won't be repulsed by me. *(Upon saying this Luisa stares fixedly at Marta.)*

MARTA. Repulsed by you! For God's sake, Luisa, don't say that!

LUISA. I say it because it's true. Where do I take a bath?

MARTA. Eat first...I didn't say you have to take a bath right away, I...

LUISA. *(Interrupting.)* Right now, Martita! Right now! That way I don't disgust you or mess up your beautiful house...*(She looks all around and then stares at Marta. She goes to her and takes her by the arm.)* Where? Martita, where?

MARTA. *(Pushed on by the Indian woman, Marta walks her to the bathroom door adjacent to the bedroom.)* I'm going to show you how the shower works.

LUISA. *(Luisa lets go of her arm, enters the bathroom, leaves the door ajar, and sticks out her head.)* But I know how, Martita, I know how.

MARTA. No, you don't. You've never seen a shower. You'll burn yourself. The water comes out boiling. *(Marta tries to enter the bathroom. Luisa pushes her and slams the door, locking it.)* Don't be stubborn! Let me in! Let me in, I tell you!

LUISA. *(Off.)* I know how, I know how.

MARTA. Crazy old loon! Luisa! Luisa! *(Sounds of the shower turning on. Marta bangs on the door but the old Indian woman does not respond.)* Oh, all right, burn yourself! What do I care. It's going to be hell getting you back to the village, you good for nothing. I bet you couldn't find your way back alone. *(Calming down.)* Luisa! How did you find my house if you've never been to Mexico City? *(Luisa does not respond. Sounds of the water running. Marta pounds on the door a few more times, then stops.)* What a strange old Indian! I've known her for years and now I know why no one in the village likes her. But how did she find the way to my house?

(The lights dim. A clock strikes the hour. Then the phone rings and the lights come back on. Enter Luisa running. She is wearing clean clothes and her hair is loose and damp. She picks up the telephone and listens attentively.)

LUISA. Hello? Martita is busy...yes, making supper...I tell you she's busy...*(Enter Marta with a tray of food in her hands, surprised at seeing Luisa talking on the telephone. She places the tray on a little table and goes to pick up the telephone.)* Yes...yes...good-bye. *(She hangs up the telephone and smiles at Marta.)*

MARTA. Why did you hang up? Luisa, why are you such a dimwit! Why did you answer the phone if you don't know how to use it?

LUISA. I know how, Martita, I know how.

MARTA. *(Laughing.)* How, if in your village there isn't a phone and this is the first time you've gone out? What happened is that you were curious and started chattering away like a parrot when you heard a voice speaking to you on the receiver. You liar! *(Laughing.)*

LUISA. *(Very serious.)* I am not a liar, Martita.

MARTA. Very well, but the next time it rings don't touch it, let me answer.

LUISA. But why? I know how to speak on the telephone. *(Marta, impatiently, picks up the telephone, disconnects it, and leaves the room. She returns shortly afterwards visibly upset.)*

MARTA. You think you know everything and yet you know nothing. I'm surprised you didn't get burned in the shower. You stayed there for so long I thought you drowned. Is that nice? Is that fair? You had me on edge all damn afternoon. Well, why don't you answer?

LUISA. The water comes out making so much noise who can hear, Martita, who can hear?

MARTA. Don't play dumb. *(The clock strikes eight.)* Eight o'clock! you spent three hours in the bathroom. Three hours! It's late...it could be Judgment Day and you wouldn't know it.

LUISA. It is Judgment Day, Martita.

MARTA. Here's your supper. I'm going to get mine. You start eating and keep still, don't cause any more trouble.

LUISA. Yes, Martita. *(Marta exits. Luisa sits on the edge of the sofa and waits with her head bowed. Enter Marta with another tray like the first. Upon seeing her Luisa stands up.)*

MARTA. What's the matter? Aren't you eating? What are you cooking up now?

LUISA. He's bad, Martita, bad!

MARTA. Ah, what a pain! Are you back to the same old song? Eat and be quiet. I'm telling you for the last time—your husband is a good man and you are the one who is possessed!

LUISA. Possessed?

MARTA. *(Seriously.)* Yes, Luisa, possessed. If you weren't you would take care of your children instead of harassing your husband.

LUISA. I don't do that. I take care of him because he is a coward.

MARTA. Coward? That takes the cake! What Julian should do is take his children's advice—leave you and go far away.

LUISA. *(Approaching Marta.)* Go far away? Leave me? *(Stares at Marta for a time and then walks away, giving her fleeting glances.)*

MARTA. Yes, leave you, because you are possessed...

LUISA. Possessed? But I only saw him two times.

MARTA. Who?

LUISA. The Evil One, Martita.

MARTA. *(Trying to keep from smiling.)* Ah, so you saw him two times already. Well watch out, because if you keep hounding Julian, when you die the devil will come after you the same way you chase after your husband.

LUISA. He's going to come after me?

MARTA. What you owe in this life you pay for in the other. That's why you'd better straighten up. Stay here with me for a time and think about what I said. *(Luisa looks at her with rancor.)* What's the matter, Luisa? Don't make crazy faces. Listen to what I tell you, crazy people are bad because they think that everyone is after them and that is why they bother people. *(Luisa doesn't answer. Marta holds out the tray for the Indian woman.)* Take your tray and go eat in your room! I thought we could eat together, but you're acting so strange, I prefer to be alone. Go on, take your tray! *(Luisa takes the tray and walks to the door.)* The second door to the left, the bed is all made up. Straighten up and be good!

LUISA. *(Sullen.)* All right, Martita. *(She exits. Marta eats and reads, smiling.)*

MARTA. *(To herself.)* Poor woman, I must have scared her, telling her she was possessed! *(All at once Marta grows somber and listens. In the hallway are heard footsteps as if someone barefoot were walking, barely audible, on the carpet. Marta alert, listens. Luisa appears at the door. Short and haggard beyond her years, smiling, her teeth white.)*

LUISA. Martita!

MARTA. Yes, Luisa.

LUISA. The first time I saw the evil one, it was before...

MARTA. Before what?

LUISA. Before I killed that woman...*(This produces a long and profound silence.)*

MARTA. You killed a woman? *(Luisa does not answer, her mouth hangs in a silly grin.)* Oh, Luisa, you say the most idiotic things!

LUISA. Yes, Martita, I killed that woman! *(Luisa starts laughing silently, only with the grimace of a laugh. Marta looks all around and tries to maintain her composure, in her silent room, away from the real world, closed off by her curtains and carpets.)* Martita, I am listening to your thoughts...*(Luisa approaches slowly and sits down on the floor near Marta.)* Fear is very loud, Martita...*(Beat.)* I saw the Evil One before I married my first husband...

MARTA. Your first husband? You had another husband? *(She looks at Luisa as if for the first time ever.)*

LUISA. Yes, Martita, I had another husband...but I saw the Evil One before that. I was at home in my yard and he was a cowboy dressed in black who breathed fire. In place of boots he wore horseshoes and when he walked sparks flew. In his hand he carried a whip which he used to flail the rocks and draw sparks. It was five o'clock in the afternoon and I started to shout: "There he is, there he is!" "Who's there?" asked my parents because they didn't see him. The Evil One heard me yelling and came walking up to me with his eyes all aflame. "There he is, there he is!" I screamed. "Who's that?" answered my parents because they couldn't see him. The Evil One started to whip me, before I could say his name...hours later I still had the shakes. That was the time when my first husband came to ask for my hand. My parents were glad to give me away to see if it would cure me...And we went to live in Mexico City...

MARTA. In Mexico City? You lived here in the city and never told me! *(Luisa fixes her gaze on Marta. Sitting on the floor, squatting like a small creature, trying to hide the flashes of malice that want to shoot out from her eyes.)*

LUISA. Oh, Martita, something deep down inside of me feels like laughing!

MARTA. I too feel like laughing.

LUISA. Not you, Martita, but something within me rises and falls, something like laughter...

MARTA. Well, go ahead and laugh, Luisa...

LUISA. Later, Martita...

MARTA. *(Nervously.)* Now, Luisa, now!

LUISA. Now? Now I am thinking about when I lived in Mexico City, with my first husband, and I had my child. But I swelled up, Martita, and three days after giving birth my husband took me to the village and left me at my parents' house. "She wasn't fat when you took her? Why do you bring her back like this?," said my parents. "Fuck all of you," he said. And he left. I never saw him again...but my parents didn't know that. After a while I said: "Look, father, I'm going to see if I can find my husband." And my father burst out crying. "Leave us the child," he begged. "Of course! Do you think I am so cold hearted?" And that's how I left my daughter with them and came here to live in Mexico City...*(Stopping her story to spy on Marta.)*

MARTA. Why are you staring at me, Luisa?

LUISA. I'm not staring at you, Martita, I see the house where I lived. There it is! *(She lifts up a skinny arm and points as though the house were present in the room.)*

MARTA. Luisa, don't bother me with this, don't tell me anymore. It's better to forget!

LUISA. That's where I lived...And that's where I met the woman! *(She becomes lost in her thoughts for a moment, then looks at Marta.)* The woman I killed.

MARTA. You killed her! And you say it so innocently? Why did you kill her?

LUISA. Because she was saying things...

MARTA. What things?

LUISA. Just things...that I was with her husband...she wished, I didn't even know him!

MARTA. You're never at fault! You're always blameless. Julian beats you because he's bad. You didn't know the dead woman's husband. Then, the woman speaks ill of you for nothing?

LUISA. Yes, Martita, just because she felt like it. I didn't know him. I would have to guess what he looked like! And she would say all kinds of things. And her tongue, Martita, always rattling off at the mouth. Always saying things. *(She scratches her head and then points with her index finger.)* "If you don't shut up, woman, you'll be talking to the point of my knife," that's what I said to her. But she didn't listen to me. Would you believe it, Martita, that she didn't listen? Then I went looking for her in the market place, where everyone goes to buy things. And it was pretty: full of onions, cilantro, limes. I waited for her off to the side, where the women who make tortillas are kneeling with their little baskets...and I saw her with her basket full of fruit and I said: "Now you're going to shut up,..." and I stabbed her with my knife...*(Silence.)*

MARTA. How heavy the air is in this room! We must open a window! *(She goes as if to rise. Luisa stops her.)*

LUISA. Sit down, Martita! Martita, it isn't the air that relieves us...I relieved that woman of her bad habits when I stuck her with my knife.

MARTA. Oh, Luisa! How could you do something so horrible? How can you bury a knife in someone?

LUISA. Why, in the belly, Martita. Where else is it softer and more welcome than in her guts? *(She pulls out a knife she had hidden in her blouse and pretends she is sticking an imaginary stomach.)* Like this! Like this! Like this! *(Luisa continues stabbing the air at an imaginary figure for several beats.)* And there she fell and I went running.

MARTA. *(Fascinated.)* You went running.

LUISA. Yes, I went running among the people in the market. And the people opened up to let me pass. My feet were light and my hair was on fire. And people were running after me. And I felt their steps gaining on me...*(Stops her story.)*

MARTA. Killing must be a terrible moment...perhaps murder has a certain magnificence...

LUISA. And I left the market and went down the street running. I still had the knife in my hand when I went into the house where they captured me. I was covered with blood!

MARTA. You didn't leave it stuck inside her?

LUISA. No, Martita, I took it out because it was mine! And I was dripping with blood. Would you believe it, Martita, it splattered all over me? *(Placing her knife on the floor, caressing the point of it. She pauses, lost in her reverie.)* Oh! We're full of blood. We're fountains, Martita, beautiful fountains...that's the way she looked, like a beautiful fountain in the market place...in the morning. See, Martita, a morning in the market place with its beautiful fountain?

MARTA. In what morning and what market place?

LUISA. One morning...in a market place...there she stayed with her turned over basket of onions and sweet smelling herbs mixed with blood.

MARTA. But what morning was her basket turned over?

LUISA. In a far away morning, Martita, very different from all the mornings. There she stayed. I ran and hid but they found me.

MARTA. And who was she?

LUISA. Ah well, who knows!

MARTA. What do you mean? What was her name?

LUISA. Who knows?

MARTA. You think I'm just dying to know her name and that's why you don't tell me, right? Well, let me say it, I don't care! Keep your dead woman!

LUISA. She was the woman who talked too much...that's why I stabbed her in the stomach with my knife.

MARTA. *(Looking at the knife.)* With that knife?

LUISA. Yes, Martita, this one. When I was captured they took it away from me. But I cried and cried so much they gave it back to me when I was set free.

MARTA. *(Mocking.)* They returned your knife?

LUISA. Yes, Martita.

MARTA. *(Laughing.)* Half-breed! Liar! You want to scare me because I told you that Julian was a good man. And I believed your fairy tales! I remember when the servants used to tell horror stories in the kitchen. If someone could see us now, with that knife on the floor! *(She laughs.)*

LUISA. Martita, I'm telling you they gave me my freedom and my knife. And when I was locked up I saw the Evil One again. *(Marta stops laughing.)*

MARTA. The Evil One?

LUISA. Yes, Martita, I saw him there again.

MARTA. Luisa, don't tell me anymore. I don't want to hear it! Why do you insist on frightening me? I said you were possessed just to scare you. I was playing. I never thought that word would open the door to the demons...

LUISA. Not demons, Martita. It was the Devil and he was painted on the wall of the prison. It was my size! And it was double headed, like a man and a woman! They gave me a whip and told me to flog it. Every day I would go and whip him, until my hand shook. And when I finished whipping it and I couldn't even move, some friend would say: "Go on, Luisa, whip him a little bit more for me!" And I would whip him again, because you have to be kind to your fellow prisoners. When they set me free I never saw it again...

MARTA. How nice, Luisa. You must have been very happy to be free of the devil and prison!

LUISA. *(With tenderness.)* No, Martita. Life with the prisoners wasn't so bad. At four o'clock we would wake up and start singing. Later we would grind the corn for the other prisoners. Then we would take a shower. That's why I told you I knew how to take showers! See, Martita, I wasn't lying. The showers in the prison were just like yours, except they weren't yellow.

MARTA. Of course, of course, Luisa, you weren't lying. What a dummy I am, my God!

LUISA. And we always had plenty to do. We also washed the kettles where they cooked the food for the prisoners...

MARTA. And how long were you there, Luisa?

LUISA. Who knows how long! Who knows...I forget what it was like to live outside. I spent all my time with the prisoners, my companions. That was my home and I never wanted for anything. I became so fond of the place that the nights and days went by like a flash. If we got sick, Martita, there were two doctors. Two of them! And they would take care of us...I was there so long that I considered it my home. *(She quiets down and curls up into a ball at Marta's feet.)*

MARTA. Don't be so melancholy, Luisa.

LUISA. We all miss the good times, Martita.

MARTA. Yes, we try to find good in everything.

LUISA. Don't believe it, Martita, don't believe it...

MARTA. Yes, Luisa, cheer up. You'll see, you'll have a good time here just like you did back then. You'll take a bath every day, you'll help out the girls, I'll take you to the movies. You'll see.

LUISA. No, it's not the same, Martita, it's not the same. There I had my friends and we were all equal in our sins. Here, what? *(Cheering up.)* I used to answer the phone. That's why I told you, Martita, that I knew how. See, Martita, I wasn't lying to you.

MARTA. No, you weren't lying.

LUISA. At night we would dance in the yard. The prisoners would get out their mandolins and guitars and we would dance. I never danced before, Martita! The life of the common people is no dance, the life of the poor is a hard walk down dirt roads, Martita. My companions knew how and showed me. They would put up my braids so "I wouldn't look so Indian" and we would dance and dance...

MARTA. I never thought prisoners could dance and entertain themselves...Did you dance a lot?

LUISA. Yes, I liked it! And there were lots of dances, Martita, lots.

MARTA. Luisa, you speak of the dances in the prison like others speak of dances in palaces.

LUISA. I talk of the dances because those were the times, Martita. *(She gets serious.)* When they told me they were going to give me my freedom I didn't want it. "What for, sir, where do you expect me to go?" And so I stayed. But then they told me again that I had to go. A woman said, "Do it, Luisa, do it!" And even though I didn't want to they made me. "And what do I do now, Doctor? I don't have a penny and don't want to live in the streets." But he said the streets are filled with money, Luisa, filled with money! And the doctor gave me enough for my ticket and the woman, who told me to take back my freedom, came to wish me farewell at the entrance to the real world. And when I saw myself on the street I got on a train and I went to my parents' house. *(She cries.)*

MARTA. Don't cry, Luisa, don't cry.

LUISA. *(Crying.)* But when I got there the house looked very strange Martita, very strange. Oh, Luisa, I said to myself, this house is no longer your home! And I would just sit thinking about my girlfriends and what they were doing...

MARTA. Poor Luisa! You really miss them that much? Well, how long did you live with them?

LUISA. With the prisoners? Who knows? But it was a long time. Didn't I tell you, Martita, that I forgot what it was like to be on the streets. When I got to my parents' house the child was already that big! *(She makes an imaginary line in the air denoting a child of twelve years.)*

MARTA. Weren't your parents glad to see you out of prison? What did they say to you?

LUISA. *(On guard.)* Nothing! How are you, daughter?

MARTA. But what did they say about your being in prison for so long? Come on, they're your parents—they must have said something.

LUISA. They never said anything about jail. Because they didn't know. No one knew! They thought I was living with my husband in Tacubaya.

MARTA. How is it possible they never knew? Don't tell me you're such a hypocrite that you never told them! What about your first husband?

LUISA. He never said anything...luckily someone killed him and he never returned to the village to tell. There are some things, Martita, that no one should know. No one knew I was in prison. Not my parents who are now dead, not Julian. When he came to ask for my hand I told him nothing. I passed as a widow and a widow I am.

MARTA. You deceived him? Poor man!

LUISA. I didn't deceive him, I just kept silent. *(A long pause.)*

MARTA. It's getting very late.

LUISA. *(Not listening to her.)* Before I left jail, my girlfriends, who loved me a lot, said: "Look, Luisa, don't ever tell anyone you killed that woman. People are bad, very bad."

MARTA. There are all kinds of people, Luisa, but who are they to judge?

LUISA. *(Looking at her fixedly.)* They knew it. That's why they warned me. "We know you'll have the urge to tell someone," they said, "your own sins oblige you to confess them. You have your sins but they're yours and no one else's. Besides that, you have the sins of the woman and between all of them they hang heavy on your soul." Did you know, Martita, that we're burdened with the sins of those we kill? That's why those men who owe two or three deaths are doubled over by the weight. "But don't say anything to anyone, Luisa, don't even tell them where you've been all these years!"

MARTA. Just me? And why didn't you confess to a priest? It would have done you a lot of good, Luisa.

LUISA. "Look," said my companions, "if you ever feel that the sins are weighing too heavy—go to the country far from the people. Seek out a leafy tree, put your arms around it, and confess. But only when you can't stand it anymore, Luisa, because it only works once." And that's what happened, Martita, time passed and I kept my secret. One day my legs started to buckle and I couldn't eat because of my sins and the sins of the dead woman, which were more than mine. They sat heavy in my stomach. One day I told Julian: "I'm going for some firewood." And I went to the forest and found a leafy tree and did what my companions told me. I put my arms around it and said: "Look tree, I've come to confess my sins, so that you may carry them for me." I stayed there four hours telling it what I had done! *(She looks at Marta who is disturbed.)*

MARTA. And the tree unburdened you of your sins?

LUISA. A long time passed before I went to see it again...but when I got there. *(She stops.)*

MARTA. When you got there, what?

LUISA. I found it all dried up, Marta. Why did it dry up?

MARTA. It dried up!

LUISA. I unburdened my sins on it and it dried up. *(Pause. Marta looks around nervously.)*

MARTA. It's midnight, Luisa, we've been talking for four hours...

LUISA. Four hours, Martita? I also spent four hours with the tree.

MARTA. *(Nervously.)* Forget everything, Luisa. I was joking when I said you were possessed. We've all done bad things...forget about it, stop living in the past. *(Luisa freezes, lost in her wild thoughts.)* Calm down, Luisa. Don't be afraid. What is there to be afraid of, if we're both here safe and sound!

LUISA. It dried up, Martita, it dried up...

MARTA. You already told me, Luisa. No need to tell me again. Calm down and go to sleep...

LUISA. How alone are we, Martita!

MARTA. Alone? Why do you say that?

LUISA. Because the girls don't return until tomorrow morning.

MARTA. So what...let's go to sleep.

LUISA. But it dried up, Martita, it dried up...

MARTA. Luisa, don't act like this, repeating things like an idiot—it dried up, it dried up. I don't know what you're trying to prove repeating this phrase. Hush up and go to sleep. You know where your room is. Go on! *(Luisa gets on her feet and picks up her knife.)* Leave the knife, Luisa!

LUISA. *(Cradling the knife.)* It's mine, Martita, mine!

MARTA. You caress it as though it were a treasure. Oh, Luisa! Do you think you'll open the doors to the palace of the mandolins and guitars where you danced with your friends with that knife? *(She stops and looks fearfully at Luisa.)*

LUISA. That's the way it was and that's the way it shall be; the key to the palaces...*(Both women look afraid now.)*

MARTA. Good night, Luisa! Do you know the door to your room?

LUISA. Yes, Martita, good night. *(She starts to leave.)*

MARTA. Sleep well.

LUISA. *(Stopping at the door.)* How very silent is this house, Martita! *(She exits.)*

(Marta sits quietly not knowing what to do, trying to straighten out some bottles on top of the dressing table. She brushes her hair and tries to smile in front of the mirror.)

MARTA. She has to be as scared as I am. How stupid it was to start telling stories like this in the middle of the night! *(She takes off her shoes, then suddenly stops and listens.)*

LUISA. *(Off.)* And it dried up, Martita, it dried up...*(Marta tenses up and tries to hear. It sounds like muffled footsteps on the carpet approaching.)*

MARTA. Luisa! Luisa! Answer, Luisa! *(Beat.)* You're going to be the death of me, Luisa! Are you sleeping as I think out loud...Come and talk to me, don't annoy me. Just because you confided in me...Oh my God, how could I be so stupid! What am I saying! Luisa! *(She stops, anxiously listening to the imaginary noises. Frightened, she goes to the bathroom door and exits, reentering a few seconds later.)* Luisa! What did you do with the key to the bathroom? The phone is far away! Why did I take it out, my God! And the door to my room has no key either! Luisa, come and talk to me, loneliness is a terrible companion! Don't stay there alone imagining terrible things. I hear your footsteps in the hallway....why don't you answer? Luisa, I know you're behind the door spying on me, I hear your breathing...*(Luisa's footsteps and the sound of her panting are heard behind the door.)* You're crazy! Now I know it. You're crazy, crazy! That's why they hate you in the village. *(Terrified, she takes her head between her hands and sways back and forth.)* And just because the tree dried up? Just because of that, to me, your friend? *(Marta looks for a way to escape with her eyes. Slowly, she opens the door to her room and Luisa's hand and foot appear.)*

LUISA. *(Still behind the door.)* That's why, Martita, that's why...

THE END

PROFANE GAMES

(The Inferno: Part of a Trilogy of Games)

by

CARLOS OLMOS

TRANSLATED FROM THE SPANISH

by

CARLOS MORTON

The English-language premier of PROFANE GAMES took place on February 22, 1991 in Dallas, Texas. It was produced by Teatro Dallas and directed by Eduardo Ruiz Savinon.

CHARACTERS

ALMA

SAUL

THE SCENE

Present-day Mexico City

(This first image of the trilogy is a dream, a foolish farce, that takes place on Christmas Eve. Time: The present. The scenography is simple: The dining room of a typical middle-class home. As the curtain rises a faint light falls on the silhouette of Saul, who is standing by the windows leading to the dining room. He speaks to someone in the garden.)

SAUL. Mother, no! Don't touch that tree. Leave it like that. It doesn't need lights. You'd better come in. It's cold outside and you'll catch your death. *(Pause.)* Why don't you get dressed? You see? The wind is starting up. Look how it stirs the trees! The ornaments are falling! And all the trouble it took you to decorate it! Oh, they're breaking! *(Another pause.)* Don't get mad. Don't make faces. It wasn't your fault...*(Saul lowers his head. Alma enters in a wheelchair. She sees Saul and wheels over by his side. She laughs and starts singing.)*

ALMA. You better watch out, you better not pout, you better not cry, I'm telling you why, Santa Claus is coming to town! *(Alma raises her arm and turns on a light switch. A change of light occurs.)*

SAUL. Why are you turning on the light? Shut it off!

ALMA. *(Spinning the wheel chair around.)*
He knows if you've been happy,
He knows if you've been sad,
He knows if you've been good or bad.
So be good for goodness sake!

SAUL. Turn them off, I tell you! Mother is dressing the trees in the garden and needs it dark! Don't you understand? You should be helping her instead of singing like a maniac.

ALMA. *(Indifferent.)* She wouldn't let me. I offered, but she wouldn't let me. *(Continuing to sing, she moves towards the Christmas tree and leaves a Christmas card on it. Saul, furious, spins the chair around and gives Alma a hard slap in the face.)*

SAUL. Listen to me when I talk to you!

ALMA. You've slapped me twenty-five times today, Saul, one more and...

SAUL. You deserve it! Take that dress off this instant!

ALMA. You asked me to wear it...!

SAUL. Well, forget it. Take it off and put on another!

ALMA. You're angry?

SAUL. Aren't I always?

ALMA. I thought today you would try and control yourself a bit. For me...and for the celebration.

SAUL. *(Taking the Christmas card from the tree.)* And this?

ALMA. Never mind.

SAUL. Writing to Santa Claus again?

ALMA. So what if I am? Who are you to stop me?

SAUL. But...it's for me? *(Happy.)* Really? For me?

ALMA. *(Pulling off a blue ornament.)* And this too.

SAUL. *(Embracing her.)* I thought you had forgotten...

ALMA. Is that why you're angry? I found the biggest, most beautiful ornament and kept it for you.

SAUL. The most beautiful?

ALMA. Check out the tree, you'll see.

SAUL. *(Fascinated.)* How did you manage to save it?

ALMA. It's the only one left from that night. All the others are new. I bought them yesterday. And now, give it to me. We'll put it up at the very top. *(She places it at the top. She smells the odor of pine.)* Ah, it smells wonderful.

SAUL. It's the smell of the forest.

ALMA. No. Of our home.

SAUL. Then it smells of sadness.

ALMA. But...you're not happy?

SAUL. Yes, but I don't feel like dancing.

ALMA. Why not? *(And now, in a natural way, Saul rises to his feet and starts an improvised dance.)* We should live life to its fullest! We're young! *(Singing.)* "You better not shout, you better not cry, you better not pout, I'm telling you why..."

SAUL. Alma, please, take off that dress.

ALMA. *(Like a spoiled little girl.)* No!

SAUL. *(Meekly.)* I beg you...

ALMA. No! Why is it that whenever I try to please you, you end up throwing it in my face? Didn't you say I looked ten years younger with it on? *(She kisses him.)* We're going to take care of each other, Saul. Even if it's just for tonight. Would you like a drink?

SAUL. Yes.

ALMA. We'll drink until we're absolutely drunk! In spite of everything, it's going to be a memorable night, don't you think!

SAUL. So memorable you wanted to spend it alone?

ALMA. It was your idea! Why blame me?

SAUL. You could have persuaded me otherwise. I'm very weak. You know that.

ALMA. *(Alma gives him a drink, returns to sit in the wheelchair, and gets ready to toast.)* Now what? Do you want me to invite them in?

SAUL. It is customary to spend Christmas among family.

ALMA. Oh? Boring ourselves to death?

SAUL. What did you make for dinner?

ALMA. What was I supposed to make? Turkey, of course!

SAUL. I think Mother is finished.

ALMA. She's been there since dark. Are you gong to bring her in now?

SAUL. *(At the window.)* Did you finish, Mummy?

ALMA. *(Changing her expression, with rage, almost in a whisper.)* That must be the signal to start! *(Throwing the cup away, she crushes the blue sphere in her hand.)*

SAUL. Idiot, what are you doing?

ALMA. What you see!

SAUL. What are you trying to do?

ALMA. What do you think? Drive you mad!

SAUL. *(Giving her another slap in the face.)* I've had it with you! It wouldn't hurt to have Mother dine with us!

ALMA. Yes, it would! I feel like poisoning her drink.

SAUL. Oh, that's the easy way out!

ALMA. What would you do?

SAUL. Probably the same thing. *(Smiling, joking.)* Now that we're play acting, tell me...thought about prison?

ALMA. You mean our home?

SAUL. You could look at it that way.

ALMA. Well it is! Can we live like other people? Are we free to leave when we feel like it? Always having to ask permission, letting others decide for us, passing our lives away...

SAUL. If it bothers you that much to dine with them, then leave. I'll think of a good excuse when they ask for you.

ALMA. You should learn to abide by your decisions. Be a little more of an adult and less of a child. This afternoon you swore to me that we would dine alone, that it was time to live an independent life, that they had to realize we're made of flesh and bone...(*Alma stops herself. She looks at him with fear. Saul smiles.*)

SAUL. So are they.

ALMA. I never said they weren't. (*Pause.*) If only we could be without them for one night.

SAUL. Don't even think about it. And lower your voice, they're liable to hear you.

ALMA. Let them! They should know the truth once and for all.

SAUL. Exactly. They have to be told, which is why I changed my mind with regards to their presence.

ALMA. (*Surprised.*) Are you serious?

SAUL. Today is our tenth anniversary, right?

ALMA. What are you plotting?

SAUL. To tell them everything.

ALMA. (*Terrified.*) Tonight?

SAUL. After dinner. If we did it before, they'd lose their appetite.

ALMA. And after I spent all morning cooking. (*Smiling.*) For you.

SAUL. Really? I thought it was for the old man.

ALMA. I did it for you! There are times when I don't even think about Father.

SAUL. You could probably count them on your fingers. You live only to please his whims.

ALMA. They are not whims! He's sick!

SAUL. Of you! He does everything he can just to keep you by his side! Don't think I haven't noticed, Alma. He's been playing sick for years just to be with you.

ALMA. (*Cynical.*) So what? You have Mother to make up for it.

SAUL. You leave her out of this!

ALMA. I'm not dragging her into it! But I'm warning you, if you want to play...

SAUL. *(Slapping her again.)* Mother is different! You have no right to insult her!

ALMA. You love her that much?

SAUL. *(Lyrically.)* More than you could ever imagine.

ALMA. I understand perfectly well, though her love will never compare with mine.

SAUL. Of course not! I'm the intense one.

ALMA. Perhaps. Although I gave you the idea for the skeletons.

SAUL. But who put it into action, eh? Who made it real?

ALMA. Both of us!

SAUL. Forget it! If our parents have someone to thank for being alive, it's me!

ALMA. It sounds like you're beginning to have second thoughts. If we tell them "that" they'll cease to exist. Everything would end, you beast!

SAUL. *(After a pause, baffled.)* I was just testing you.

ALMA. That won't get you anywhere. Now, if you're still up to it, go get her.

SAUL. It's not time yet. Too early.

ALMA. I thought you were in a hurry.

SAUL. *(Exploding.)* It's too early!

ALMA. As you wish. *(Long pause. Alma finishes her drink, goes to the dining room and sets the plates. Saul, facing the audience, looks at a fixed point in the distance.)*

SAUL. What a beautiful expression you had when you were young. You were bliss incarnate. Who were you thinking of?

ALMA. Father. He didn't even "know" you then.

SAUL. I told you not to interrupt me when I'm talking to her!

ALMA. I can't help it. I should let you sit there the rest of your life talking to a painting. Why not go to her room and tell her that. But, of course, you're such a coward, you'd rather whisper to the wind.

SAUL. *(Referring to the mother.)* It's better than talking to the ruins.

ALMA. Are you afraid?

SAUL. Nauseous.

ALMA. Since when? *(Smiling perversely.)* You made love to her, didn't you?

SAUL. Jealous?

ALMA. I made love to Father. Only once. But I did it.

SAUL. It's not true. You're only saying that to hurt me.

ALMA. After you confessed to me, I said, "Alma, what's good for the goose is good for the gander." And so, I did it too.

SAUL. How did it feel?

ALMA. Don't get morbid.

SAUL. *(Laughs.)* It's not true, Alma, absolutely not! You're not capable of something like that!

ALMA. How do you know? Schizophrenia is contagious, little brother.

SAUL. *(He hits her six times.)* Imbecile, we're talking about necrophilia! If you want to insult me, at least do it in good taste!

ALMA. Well, I did make love to him! I did! *(Looking at him with hatred.)* You're going to pay for this! *(Practically spitting in his face.)* Oedipus!

SAUL. *(Enraged like a child.)* Electra! *(He sits down in the same place. Alma begins to cry.)* You better shut up! You'll never come close to being like Mother!

ALMA. I'm her spitting image, even if it galls you.

SAUL. Hardly! Mother was much more beautiful! Next to her you're a caricature.

ALMA. Except that for now you have to settle for me, right?

SAUL. I'm sick and tired of you too! You'll never be like her. Not even by putting on her clothes. Mother was a nymph, a princess.

ALMA. Don't exaggerate.

SAUL. She was beautiful, but the sickness wasted her. *(Sighing.)* Ah, if only Goya had known her.

ALMA. Did you see her when she was in pain? With her mouth all twisted, and her eyes popping out of her head! She looked like an old hag!

SAUL. You're talking that way because Father preferred her. You were always playing second fiddle.

ALMA. You're just saying that!

SAUL. That's what you said in bed.

ALMA. You've said worst things, but at least I have the delicacy not to repeat them.

SAUL. Delicacy, you? You're a foul-mouthed...

ALMA. You forced me, Saul!

SAUL. Don't threaten me, Alma! *(Looking at her.)* Perhaps we should each go our own way.

ALMA. *(Surprised.)* Are you serious?

SAUL. Absolutely.

ALMA. After so many years?

SAUL. Ten to be exact.

ALMA. *(Challenging.)* You think it'll be that easy?

SAUL. Very.

ALMA. So what are you going to do? Kill me?

SAUL. Something more difficult—forget you.

ALMA. *(Harassing him.)* You think any other woman would put up with you?

SAUL. I haven't anyone else in mind. I want to live alone. Do you understand? *(Firmly.)* I want you to leave.

ALMA. Oh, how cute. Now it turns out I'm the one who should leave.

SAUL. Take what you want. Including Father.

ALMA. Are you mad?

SAUL. The house is mine and you're a guest who's overstayed her welcome...

ALMA. You never said that, even when you refused to bury her.

SAUL. At least she never stank! She was a saint!

ALMA. Do you think you can get rid of me that easy? You think Father will let you? You're something else. Run me out of the house! After you begged me to stay with you! To help you stand the pain of living without them! After you turned me into a whore!

SAUL. Alma!

ALMA. That's what I am thanks to you! Do you think a decent girl would play these games? Do you think I can go out and face the world? Telling everyone that I've returned after years of being shut up, my brother's lover? Taking care of and dressing two skeletons just so the little master could feel protected or punished? Do you think this is easy?

SAUL. I only want to...

ALMA. Betray me! Throw me in the trash after you've used up the best part of me!

SAUL. You did it of your own free will, Alma. No one forced you.

ALMA. Because you promised it would only be for a few days, while you tried to forget the odor of death.

SAUL. But it was you who later took advantage of the situation to lay traps for me.

ALMA. You asked for it! If I hadn't gone along with it, you would have committed suicide. You threatened to. Didn't you trick me by locking yourself up in your room and playing dead?

SAUL. I wanted to know if I could count on you. That was all.

ALMA. I was there for you. But when we got to the nitty gritty...

SAUL. Shut up!

ALMA. Are you ashamed?

SAUL. I did it for you!

ALMA. Oh yes! Did you think of me the first time we did it?

SAUL. I tried and failed. I only wanted to see other things, feel the impossible.

ALMA. You should have tried to imagine them. Won them over with fantasy. Something, I don't know, less dangerous.

SAUL. I had to get it all out! Explode! It was the only way not to contaminate myself, letting desire take its course. Wishing, always wishing. Alma, we can still stop it, if we want to!

ALMA. Not me!

SAUL. Why not?

ALMA. It's gotten to be a habit. I can't help but looking at you like I would a man. What are you afraid of?

SAUL. Them.

ALMA. They'll never find out.

SAUL. But there are times when they look at me, reproachfully, as if I had committed a crime.

ALMA. They look at you?

SAUL. *(In anguish.)* I think they're alive! They watch us!

ALMA. Are you insane? How can a bunch of bones be alive?

SAUL. You should take a good look at them, Sister!

ALMA. I have. Don't forget that I care for them daily, dust them, change their clothes, and lately, even do mother's hair.

SAUL. Are you sure they're not alive?

ALMA. *(Firmly.)* How many times do I have to tell you, those bones are not them!

SAUL. One more reminder like that and I'll split your face open! *(Saul has picked up a knife from the table.)*

ALMA. *(Trying to calm him.)* You don't have to get all excited. I'm just trying to show you things as they really are.

SAUL. But not that way!

ALMA. It's only a game! But don't take it so seriously! Try to be more realistic. Saul, live for the moment! Let yourself go!

SAUL. I don't have to!

ALMA. Well, I don't have to listen to your list of fears! Try and control your paranoia!

SAUL. If that's what you call the pain of living a vile abstraction...

ALMA. *(Fed up.)* What philosopher are you reading now?

SAUL. I'm only thinking out loud, you imbecile!

ALMA. Do it in our dear mother's bedroom! Don't bother me any more! Go and tell her everything!

SAUL. You think me so cynical?

ALMA. You try it every Christmas.

SAUL. You always prevent me.

ALMA. It seems to be very bad taste to mix Santa Claus with incest.

SAUL. I proposed doing it during New Year's day but you said no!

ALMA. One has to respect tradition. Come on, look me in the face, tell me you honestly want to end it all!

SAUL. *(Smiling.)* You don't.

ALMA. It'd be a lot easier for me. I'm a woman, a victim. We're notorious for being frail. If worse comes to worse, it's not my fault. You're the one who's insane.

SAUL. You promised we would both confess! You said you were ready!

ALMA. Come on, Saul, don't torture yourself. Let fate decide. I wanted us to have a peaceful evening. Weren't you happy to get my Christmas card? Look at the tree. It's been ten years since it was decorated. If we don't remember, who will? *(Kissing him.)* I'm willing to do anything you want, so as not to lose you. Not that. The only thing I have is you. It would be a disaster, after all this time, to find another meaning to life. *(Transition.)* Father told me yesterday that I'm getting old, which made Mother very happy. Is it true, Saul, am I getting old?

SAUL. Yesterday?

ALMA. When we went for the gifts. You don't remember? I thought you heard him.

SAUL. Maybe I was thinking of something else.

ALMA. Perhaps. Because you were touching my knees under the table with your shoes.

SAUL. That's right! And they almost found us out!

ALMA. You little devil. *(Caressing him.)* Don't forget you have to give me the right signals, so I can be alert.

SAUL. It's not the same thing. I love to take you by surprise.

ALMA. Oh, Nicolás, Nicolás!

(Change of lights. They both fall to the floor and initiate an erotic game of nervous giggles and suggestive movements.)

ALMA. We should be more discreet, old lover.

SAUL. Venturina, my adorable, Venturina.

ALMA. Oh, you're hurting me, Nicolás! Control yourself!

SAUL. I'd love to have your flesh next to mine, for ever and ever. Dream atop your nakedness as one.

ALMA. Dream on.

SAUL. Alma, my love. We're pure, we're innocent!

ALMA. In the end this is what I wanted! *(They kiss.)*

SAUL. I think it's raining.

ALMA. It's not August. It can't rain because it's not August and my dress is white, not green.

SAUL. You look bewitching tonight, Venturina. You look like...

ALMA. *(Quickly.)* Like myself! See the ocean, Nicolás? Tell me that you see it. Tomorrow we will go to the beach, throw ourselves on the sand...

SAUL. Alone?

ALMA. Yes. The children hardly ever let us go out.

SAUL. Shhhh. Quiet! They're in the living room! I don't know why they whisper so. *(Pause.)* When I was in the garden with you just now, decorating the cypresses, I got the impression that Saul was watching us.

ALMA. *(Laughing.)* He wanted to help me with the artificial snow.

SAUL. But I saw his face reflected on the window. Such a strange look.

ALMA. He was angry. That's all. I wouldn't let him go out. Because of the wind. And you know what? Not one bulb remained in place.

SAUL. That boy...

ALMA. He's no problem. If you observe closely, Alma is more special. I almost perceive a mixture of scorn and evil in those eyes.

SAUL. Evil? How can there be evil in someone who looks so much like you? *(Saul gets up.)*

ALMA. *(Perplexed.)* Where are you going?

SAUL. It's getting late. They're waiting for us. And Saul told me he has something important to tell us.

ALMA. *(Tormented.)* But you can't go yet. They haven't invited us!

SAUL. But we're not strangers...

ALMA. If we pretended to be sick...

SAUL. *(Firmly.)* No, tonight is the night!

ALMA. *(Frantically heading him off.)* You won't be able to say anything! Your voice will dry up! You won't confess a thing! Father will start talking about my wedding! My imminent wedding! You haven't forgotten that, have you?

SAUL. Tonight, after dinner.

ALMA. After dinner we'll dance! Celebrate the birth of Christ! Give thanks to the heavens for allowing us to live one more year and then...

SAUL. The party will end and in the middle of everything...

ALMA. You'll recite a religious poem. *(Laughing.)* That's all!

SAUL. Don't laugh like that!

ALMA. I'll laugh the way I want to! Mother's heart is not well. She could die of fright. They'll blame you. Her curse would be upon you forever.

SAUL. But outside, in the street, I could feel the sun, people, the rush!

ALMA. Of remorse for having killed her?

SAUL. So what? I will have said it! I'll have done it!

ALMA. Well, they won't come!

SAUL. What?

ALMA. You heard! They won't come! Father isn't feeling well.

SAUL. You can't stop it Alma! I'll make myself heard!

ALMA. *(Struggling.)* Please, restrain yourself! Think of what will become of me without my family!

SAUL. Every man for himself! *(Another change of lights. Music comes on. Saul takes the wheelchair and exits. Alma tries to stop him but, upon hearing some distant bells, spins and says in a murmur.)*

ALMA. We won't tell them! They don't need to know our secret! They don't have to forgive us for anything. If only a miracle would occur...*(And now the bells are heard more loudly.)* It's ten o'clock! Within a few hours you'll be born. Tonight, I feel a light inside me. Voices of dead children. Shadows that multiply themselves. Who do I fear, my God, who?

(Saul enters. A female skeleton dressed in an evening gown appears seated in the wheelchair, a white wig over her skull. Saul seems very satisfied.)

(Author's note: During the premiere of the play manikins of mummified appearance were used in place of skeletons. The actors moved them like puppets. This permitted a wide range of theatrical possibilities. In the following scenes, the spectacle should be emphasized through attitude, voice and gesture, rather than grotesque exaggeration. For Alma and Saul the game is literally child's play, and their capacity to convince us is essential to the farce.)

ALMA. Good evening, Mummy.

SAUL. Good evening, Daughter. Go for your father.

ALMA. Would you like some champagne?

SAUL. The doctor has forbidden it.

ALMA. One glass won't do any harm.

SAUL. (To his mother.) I advise you not to drink anything. In your delicate state...

ALMA. You're right. We wouldn't want her to expire before her time.

SAUL. I'll get even with you when you bring your old man.

ALMA. Father doesn't cause such a stink!

SAUL. *(Like the mother.)* This night always makes me very sentimental. Do what your brother says, dear. You see how your father refuses to move a foot without you.

ALMA. *(To Saul.)* Well, at least you recognize that. *(Alma gives the glass to Saul and exits. Saul talks while he places the glass in his mother's hand.)*

SAUL. You know, I haven't been feeling well lately. I have a pain here, in my throat. It's probably from smoking too much. The doctor warned me, but... *(As Saul, in a rapid transition.)* Try to stop smoking for just one day. The cancer will eat you up before you know it, Mother. You look very pretty tonight. A little bit on the thin side, but it looks as if the years haven't touched you at all. Father should be very proud. And me too. Not everyone has such a singular mother. Why don't you dye your hair? You'd look great as a blond. Even though your grey hair looks utterly charming. You're absolutely marvelous! I even feel like dancing with you! *(Taking her hand.)* May I have this dance, madame? *(Taking the skeleton and dancing a waltz.)* Madame, you're as light as a feather! *(Enter Alma with the other skeleton. The spectacle of Saul dancing with the mother is overwhelming. Alma stops to observe them. Alma's skeleton is dressed in tails and cane.*

ALMA. *(Alma speaks as the father.)* So, you're already enjoying yourselves, eh?

SAUL. *(Natural.)* Come on, you hardly ever let me have a moment with her, old man.

ALMA. Daddy, would you like something to drink?

SAUL. Don't sit him there! That's Mother's place!

ALMA. This is my father's chair!

SAUL. But Mother was here first! He can sit somewhere else. Now then, lady, sit yourself right down. *(He takes the skeleton over to the wheelchair.)*

ALMA. *(Sitting the father down in front of the mother.)* Just you wait, Daddy, the turkey turned out delicious.

SAUL. You went to all that trouble, daughter dear? We have the maid for that.

ALMA. *(To the father.)* Do you like how I set the table?

SAUL. I would have done it better.

ALMA. No you wouldn't, Mother. You don't have the strength.

SAUL. Why are you like that, Mother? A woman should learn how to keep house, because later she won't know a darn thing.

ALMA. If I go into the kitchen it's to make myself a more well-rounded person. Right, Saul?

SAUL. Why do you ask me? Your future husband should thank you.

ALMA. Don't talk about that!

SAUL. *(Moving the skull of his skeleton over to the left side.)* To think that this is the last Christmas we'll ever spend together!

ALMA. Venturina, please! Don't get sentimental now! That only happens to you on New Year's Eve.

SAUL. You understand, don't you Son? It's terrible watching the little ones grow up. One is left so alone after they leave.

ALMA. I hope you'll come and visit us often, Alma.

SAUL. Of course she will, Father, she can't stand to be without you!

ALMA. And what daughter can get used to living away from home all at once? It's easy for a man.

SAUL. It all depends.

ALMA. On what? When I got married to your Mother...

SAUL. You weren't in love with your Mother! *(A long pause.)* Sister, would you like to dance?

ALMA. Leave me alone!

SAUL. Are you angry?

ALMA. I'm angry because you don't show me any respect!

SAUL. It's just that my love for Big Mama is so overpowering.

ALMA. Do you have to say it every minute! Do you want to ruin everything?

SAUL. I am going to make a clean breast of it and nothing can change my mind.

ALMA. But not that way. Go slow, like always. Don't confuse everybody.

SAUL. I'm going to have to change the order of things! We'd better tell them before dinner.

ALMA. What's your hurry? Can't you make your statement later?

SAUL. So nothing will happen? We'll be stuck in the dining room with nothing to do, except eat and eat.

ALMA. It would be better to let them dine in peace. Don't you feel sorry for them? What right do we have to...

SAUL. To live freely! Isn't that enough!

ALMA. *(Looking at the skeletons.)* The poor babies! They look so content, so full of life. Why don't you leave everything to me?

SAUL. I gave you the opportunity five years ago and all you did was start to cry. No, let's go. Serve dinner!

ALMA. I want to be there when it happens!

SAUL. Think you can take it?

ALMA. I'll try!

SAUL. *(Saul takes her by the hand, making believe that they've finished dancing.)* Mummy, don't you think Alma dances well? My future brother-in-law doesn't realize what a jewel she is.

ALMA. Don't exaggerate. What's happening is that...

SAUL. The time has arrived!

ALMA. Why so secretive, you naughty children? Is it the surprise? Venchu can't wait to hear what you have to say.

SAUL. Don't tell me you want to get married too, Saulito...

ALMA. No! A man should savor his bachelorhood. Saul is very young and to do something as stupid as that...

SAUL. What's the matter, Son, why are you so nervous?

ALMA. This is one of his little melodramas...

SAUL. I am very serious, I assure you.

ALMA. *(With her skeleton.)* What's wrong? Say what you're going to say and be quick about it. I'm dying of hunger!

SAUL. *(Trapped, he seizes his skeleton and confronts Almas'.)* Please, Nick, it's not the end of the world. The boy is only passing through one of his phases.

ALMA. Always the same! You with your tantrums, charades and little scenes! When are you going to grow up? If you want to tell us something...

SAUL. He'll tell you, don't get angry. What's the matter, Son? You're all pale and sweaty. What's wrong?

ALMA. Nothing! He's making a mountain out of a mole hill! Don't pay attention to him!

SAUL. Come on Son, out with it. What's the matter? Have you done something behind our backs?

ALMA. How could he! You keep track of him day and night! He even has to ask permission to go to the bathroom.

SAUL. Alma!

ALMA. It's Father talking, you idiot!

SAUL. It's the way you said it...

ALMA. Your attitude obviously irritates him. How do you expect him to be civil? Father was very emotional!

SAUL. But don't use that as an excuse to insult me!

ALMA. Sit down, Daddy, leave everything to me. I'll calm him down and we can eat in peace, you'll see.

SAUL. It won't work. What I have to say is mind boggling!

ALMA. Leave well enough alone, let it be our secret!

SAUL. It's not enough that we know it! There are things that deserve punishment!

ALMA. Punish yourself, masochist!

SAUL. Imbecile! You know nothing of the classics. You'll never be able to purge yourself!

ALMA. To tell you the truth, I like living this hell!

SAUL. Then, act dignified! Stop being so "Freudian" and analyzing our sex life! Sometimes things have to be explained in other ways!

ALMA. There's a time and a place for everything. No one can judge us. We're living the life we chose for ourselves, Saul. We're happy this way!

SAUL. What are you talking about! Come on, out with it...

ALMA. Nothing! It's just that Saul wants to leave the house. That's all! *(Lifting up her skeleton.)* Aha! So that was it!

SAUL. *(Furiously, he picks up the father and throws him across the room with a crash.)* You're a pig like all the others!

ALMA. *(Running to her father, lifting him up.)* If you do that again!

SAUL. Let him lie there!

ALMA. How could you? Papa, Papa! Are you hurt? Answer me! You wretch! You almost broke his neck! *(Frightened.)* Look, blood! He's bleeding!

SAUL. Oh, he's alright!

ALMA. He's moaning.

SAUL. Oh, put some rubbing alcohol and a band-aid on him and he'll be fine.

ALMA. How inconsiderate of you!

SAUL. It takes more than that to bring him down.

ALMA. How can you say that Mother? One would think you wished him dead.

SAUL. So what? Then we would be tit-for-tat, wouldn't we, Alma?

ALMA. What are you trying to say?

SAUL. That Saulito told me what you confessed last Christmas. Yes, don't act surprised. When you came at me from behind with a pillow!

ALMA. That's a lie! I never said that!

SAUL. Don't interrupt me! Remember that I am your mother!

ALMA. If you're going to use that to...

SAUL. Put your father in that chair and forget about him. Throw champagne in his face and see how quickly he comes too.

ALMA. Just this once...

SAUL. Just this once, shut up! You have your skeleton in the closet, I have mine!

ALMA. If I go out for a Band-Aid, you're liable to twist his neck. I know you!

SAUL. You'd better take back what you said before he comes to.

ALMA. I will not! I meant what I said!

SAUL. Is it true? Are you really leaving us, Saulito?

ALMA. Of course he is, Mother! I told you! Deep down inside he's despicable! Who could be giving him all this bad advice! After we gave him everything!

SAUL. We buy you everything you want. We helped you with your career. God knows how we sacrificed!

ALMA. He should have gotten his degree long ago! He would have been a doctor by now! A fine outstanding citizen! Not a good for nothing!

SAUL. That's enough of this! Stop it!

ALMA. We haven't eaten yet, honey buns. Do you think I'm going to go on with an empty stomach after this scene?

SAUL. I don't feel like eating!

ALMA. Fine!

SAUL. Did you hear what I said, I said I won't eat...

ALMA. If you think I'm going to beg you, you're mistaken. It's always: Is something the matter, sonny boy? What's wrong, my love? Oh, the little prince is on his high horse! Forget it! If you want to go, there's the door! But it you leave me, you'll be sorry.

SAUL. I'll take Mother with me! You will come, won't you, Mummy? We'll go to a restaurant, mix with the people, and leave this one here with her serpent's tongue...

ALMA. If you're going, leave right now! Go on! The key is in the drawer.

SAUL. *(Taking his skeleton.)* Come on, Big Mama!

ALMA. Are you crazy? How are you going to take "that" out on the street?

SAUL. You don't think I will?

ALMA. There are a lot of people out there, Saul!

SAUL. So what?

ALMA. *(With authority.)* You leave Mother where she was!

SAUL. On one condition.

ALMA. Yes, yes, what ever you want. *(Thinking it over.)* Except for that!

SAUL. I hadn't thought of that, although it's not a bad idea. *(Lifting up his mother's skirt.)*

ALMA. But it's disrespectful.

SAUL. To them, or their memory? Look! She has nice legs.

ALMA. Don't be a pig! It's only a game!

SAUL. Which you've made into reality! Don't you see we have to tell the truth? In the name of decency...

ALMA. *(Interrupting him.)* I don't want it to end! No, I can't think of life without them!

SAUL. They don't exist anymore. We "killed" them over ten years ago, remember?

ALMA. That's not true! It wasn't our fault!

SAUL. I'm not sure about that.

ALMA. What I told you last Christmas Eve was a lie. I never thought of murdering anyone.

SAUL. Are you sure?

ALMA. It's something you do when you're bored. Tedium has always been our worst enemy!

SAUL. Don't get lyrical; confess!

ALMA. It was a dream! I had to tell somebody! Believe me!

SAUL. But you wished it was real, right?

ALMA. Is it a crime to wish for something?

SAUL. Perhaps. The other paths, possibilities—are out of our control.

ALMA. What is it you want? We have no other choice. I, for one, don't have anywhere to hide. We're the only two people in the world. People without secrets aren't worth anything. You and I share one of the most beautiful ones. We shall never have a secret so radiant, so intense. Why betray it?

SAUL. We've laughed behind their backs more than enough. It's time for them to confront their creation.

ALMA. If only they were alive.

SAUL. They are alive! The only question is—where do we start? They have to listen over and over again! Until they're sick of it! Feel themselves going mad every time they remember! That will be our revenge! Boom! Explosions! Boom! They know it!

ALMA. Boom! We fail!

SAUL. It won't fail! Go ahead, serve dinner, try to mimic each gesture, every word! Tonight you must recall everything! That's our victory! Keep all the pieces of the jigsaw puzzle! We must reconstruct everything! We have to make them unforgettable!

ALMA. *(Inspecting her father's skull.)* Look! His wound healed!

SAUL. Didn't I tell you? That's as far as it would go. Oh, he loves a good show. He's O.K. Go on, take his drink and let's have dinner. Let's enjoy ourselves.

ALMA. *(Going to the dining room.)* After all, it is the most important holiday of all. Come, Daddy, here's your seat, Mother, over there. We'll sit here. Everything is delicious, Daddy, you'll love it.

SAUL. Mummy, would you like me to open the windows?

ALMA. If you like. Well, let's toast. May every Christmas be like this one! Cheers! *(She drinks.)* Don't drink any more. Venturina, it's bad for you. And it's so difficult to find a doctor tonight.

SAUL. I'll be with God. I'll be gone before you know it. The truth is that every day I feel stronger, more capable of coping. And when the will to live is there...

ALMA. That's when you're most likely to end it all, Venchu.

SAUL. Why talk about that right now?

ALMA. It's true, Father. When your time comes...

SAUL. Then let's set the clock and start all over again. Give me some salad!

ALMA. *(Serving it.)* Did you like your gift, Mummy?

SAUL. *(Annoyed.)* A lot, dear. Thanks. Pass me the salt, Nicolás.

ALMA. I always buy you the best, but it seems you never appreciate it.

SAUL. Oh, Alma. Don't start. What do you want? You have the bad luck to give me what I like the least. I appreciate it, I'm thankful, but...Nicolás, didn't you hear me? Pass the salt!

ALMA. *(Giving her the salt shaker.)* You don't look a gift horse in the mouth. Saul knows I don't like bathrobes, and yet, he buys me one.

SAUL. You don't have to wear it.

ALMA. If you don't want to give me anything, why bother?

SAUL. Force of habit.

ALMA. You mean, you "felt obligated."

SAUL. Same thing. *(Pause.)* Forget this part, Alma. It's not true. No one remembered the presents that night. It wasn't a topic of conversation.

ALMA. *(Uncomfortable.)* As you wish. I hope you give me the wrong cue, so you can see what it feels like to be cut off. *(Alma and Saul eat ceremoniously. No words for several seconds, only continuous looks.)* At this hour all the churches on earth are lit up and filled with the faithful.

SAUL. We'll go later.

ALMA. The flowers, the smell of candles and sacred music, make me feel blessed.

SAUL. Father, do you want to come with us?

ALMA. *(Engrossed.)* This is the only time of year when I recall the good old days, old friends, and places...and the Lord.

SAUL. Do you want to go with us or not?

ALMA. No. I'll go with your mother tomorrow. *(Transition.)* Will you let me borrow your veil, Mummy?

SAUL. Go ahead, take it.

ALMA. *(Kissing it.)* Thank you.

SAUL. You're welcome. *(Transition.)* The turkey was delicious.

ALMA. *(Taking hold of Saul's hand.)* Why don't we take some photographs?

SAUL. *(Waving her mother's hand.)* Yes, dear, really. Go for the camera. *(Saul gets up.)*

ALMA. Wait! Let me fix my hair!

SAUL. *(Saul has pulled out the camera.)* Stand up and hold the drink in your hand! That's it! *(The flash from the camera falls on Alma and the skeletons.)* O.K. Now with Father! Smile!

ALMA. Come one, Daddy, smile. Now, one of the two of us, no?

SAUL. Wait. We have to get the table. Ready!

ALMA. Oh no, Saul, I'm going to come out with my eyes closed like last time!

SAUL. Mummy will come out perfect! She photographs so well!

ALMA. She's the most photogenic of us all. Come on, let's have it! Get ready. Hold it!

SAUL. Mother, let's get your profile. Daddy, over there...*(Saul pushes his father's skeleton.)*

ALMA. Daddy, what's wrong? What happened, Saul?

SAUL. I don't know. I don't think he feels very well.

ALMA. Papa...

SAUL. He had too much to drink, Son. Nicolás, behave yourself!

ALMA. We'd better take to his room.

SAUL. *(Staring at Alma and whispering.)* You don't want him to hear it?

ALMA. He's about ready to fall asleep.

SAUL. Would you prefer that this part remain as always?

ALMA. Yes. That way we only have to deal with Mother...it'll be easier.

SAUL. Children, whispering in front of others is bad manners!

ALMA. It's a surprise, Mummy. *(To Saul.)* I'll take him. And don't say anything until I return! O.K. Dad, put your arm around my neck. That's it!

SAUL. *(Laughing.)* It's funny seeing Dad drunk!

ALMA. You should help me. He's heavy.

SAUL. I can't wait until we develop these photos!

ALMA. Develop this argument first and stop worrying about...

SAUL. What argument? What's Alma talking about, Saul? *(Alma smiles and exits. Saul is alone. He looks over the dining room with infinite sadness. We see grief on his face, which he then covers with his hands.)*

ALMA. Did you do it? *(Saul shakes his head. Alma talks to him as the mother.)* What's the matter, Son? What were you going to say? Is there something you don't want to tell me?

SAUL. *(Desperately.)* I'm not playing games, Alma!

ALMA. But you did the same thing earlier that evening...

SAUL. Sometimes I can't help myself. I think I'm going crazy.

ALMA. Saul, my love, let's go to bed and rest up...

SAUL. Absolutely not! It has to come out! This is the time!

ALMA. For what? Our burial? I haven't been able to feel a moment of tenderness. Last year we said the right things, cast knowing glances, caressed each other, but now...

SAUL. Now is the time to put the pieces together! We have to cleanse ourselves! We have to live! Come, help me. Both of us have to do it. *(Saul takes the mother over to the sofa.)* I'm glad Father isn't with us. It's something we've been wanting to tell you for a long time.

ALMA. You see how hard this is. Waiting a little more won't hurt. Do you realize it's been thirteen years?

SAUL. Ten.

ALMA. Thirteen.

SAUL. That's bad luck, Saulito! Give me another drink!

ALMA. You've had enough! It's now or never! To the bitter end!

SAUL. It would be better if you drank everything...in cold blood.

ALMA. Why do you look at me like that? You're not the first one this has happened to.

SAUL. Or the last.

ALMA. Calm down. Don't get excited!

SAUL. Children, please! Are we going to start this again...

ALMA. No, let's begin with the truth!

SAUL. Because you always thought your Son was an angel...

ALMA. It's no wonder he grew wings...

SAUL. And so I started to fly without your knowledge...

ALMA. Remember, even as children you noticed it.

SAUL. I thought you were going to kill me!

ALMA. In a manner of speaking.

SAUL. It started one day, when I was twelve years old.

ALMA. And I was thirteen...imagine!

SAUL. Or twenty...fifty...a thousand!

ALMA. You and Father had gone out.

SAUL. And we stayed at home. My sister always liked it when it rained.

ALMA. Yes, it was raining. I put on that blue dress, the one you wore in your youth. Saul felt an irresistible urge to put on Father's tuxedo...

SAUL. Much like the one he has on now.

ALMA. The same one. He looked so handsome! They looked so much alike!

SAUL. Alma started to dance. *(Clavichord music starts playing.)*

ALMA. *(The lights recreate the image of Alma dancing like a shadow against the walls.)* I was very happy.

SAUL. Then, I approached her and uttered your name. Yes, your name. Venturina, my adorable Venturina...

ALMA. I stopped, surprised. I realized that Saul was mistaking me.

SAUL. For my own mother.

ALMA. As he smiled, a very strange feeling came over me. He was Father! He looked exactly like Father! For the first time I felt fear...the fear of seeing a monster known only in my dreams...Saul looked knowingly at me and I...recognized his desire...and accepted it.

SAUL. We drank. The rain kept on. You can't imagine! It was a dull, dense sound. An August afternoon...with Alma in my arms weeping, in the living room, with your green dress and Father's tuxedo covering us...

ALMA. *(Somewhat slow to switch to the mother.)* What are you saying? *(Pause. For the first time the two of them just stand there looking at the skeletons and at each other repeatedly, not knowing what to say.)*

SAUL. *(Sitting down next to the skeleton.)* How could you do that to your brother!

ALMA. That's nothing! Wait until you hear the rest...

SAUL. What else happened?

ALMA. We've been acting out...that afternoon...ever since...calling ourselves Venturina and Nicolás.

SAUL. You're going to pay for this, you filthy...

ALMA. Oh, we are paying for it!

SAUL. *(Making the skeleton's arm point in an emphatic gesture.)* Leave my house! Go, Saul, go!

ALMA. What?

SAUL. That's what you deserve...you pervert! Get out of here! Take your things and leave!

ALMA. So, that's it! Is that the reason you wanted to confess?

SAUL. But, Mother, I don't want...

ALMA. You just want to leave!

SAUL. Very well! If that's what you want, I'll go.

ALMA. *(Screaming and leaving the scene for a moment.)* Father, Father, something horrible has happened! You won't believe it! *(Saul tries to leave, but Alma comes back with the father to confront him.)* Is it true what your sister says? *(Saul keeps trying to leave but Alma, putting down the father, hangs onto his neck, screaming furiously.)* You'll leave over my dead body!

SAUL. Let go of me! You're choking me, Alma! Let go! *(He breaks her strangle hold and runs over to the father's skeleton.)* You're the cause of this! It's you or me! *(Starts choking the father.)*

ALMA. *(Choking herself.)* Is this what I created! A monster! Don't kill me! Alma, don't let him kill me! Alma, help! *(Saul throws the father's skeleton down, and leans against the wall, out of breath.)* Assassin! Murderer! I'll turn you in! I'll tell them you killed him!

SAUL. Don't yell!

ALMA. *(Taking hold of the mother's skeleton.)* You'll give no orders here! From now on I'm in charge!

SAUL. What are you going to do?

ALMA. Do you think I'm going to take this lying down?

SAUL. If you touch her, I'll kill you!

ALMA. Then the deal is off! If Mother doesn't die, neither will he! Do you understand? It's all or nothing!

SAUL. I'm not going to bring that old bastard back to life! *(Yanking the mother's skeleton away from her.)*

ALMA. Give it back! Give her back to me!

SAUL. Son, what's going on? Help me!

ALMA. It's easy to talk for her, isn't it? But how can I speak for a dead man?

SAUL. Oh, let him die!

ALMA. If you want to end this, give me your skeleton! I'm going to do to it what you did to mine!

SAUL. *(Defeated, he gives it up.)* Just promise she won't suffer.

ALMA. It'll be easy...with a pillow...just like in the dream.

SAUL. Isn't there a quicker way?

ALMA. Asphyxiation is painless.

SAUL. We have a pistol!

ALMA. I'm afraid of firearms!

SAUL. If only the house had rafters...

ALMA. Hanging would be worse. Besides, it's so cruel. No, no, the pillow is the only way.

SAUL. I think I'm going to regret this.

ALMA. Not me! This is what we wanted! This is it! Wait a minute. I'll go get the big pillow. *(Alma leaves. Saul runs to the mother and kisses her bones. He lets out a scream. Alma returns.)* What's the matter? What happened?

SAUL. I don't know, it wasn't me. It was her. She just let out a scream. *(Shaking mother.)* Mother, mother, answer me!

ALMA. For God's sake, what's the matter with her?

SAUL. Alma...she's not breathing!

ALMA. *(Putting a hand on her mouth.)* It's not possible!

SAUL. She has no heartbeat!

ALMA. *(Throwing the pillow down dejectedly.)* All right, you win.

SAUL. It's getting late. It must be close to midnight. The bells are going to chime any moment. Remember, ten years ago, Alma, we used to get all dressed up and go out...

ALMA. Go, Saul, go, you're free. You've taken everything away from me, Saul, every last thing. *(Saul goes for the father, but Alma holds him back, wiping away her tears.)* Don't touch him! Now they're really dead! Dead forever! They don't belong to you now! It's over!

SAUL. If only we were capable of forgiving. Don't you feel useless? I thought love needed to be redeemed.

ALMA. Redeemed from what?

SAUL. From us.

ALMA. What are you trying to say?

SAUL. We fouled it up, we're the ones who made it putrid.

ALMA. My love doesn't stink!

SAUL. I always felt that something was decomposing bit by bit. Now I understand what it was...it was love, Alma, love.

ALMA. But I am capable of love. If there is something pure about me, that's it.

SAUL. Pure? How many lies did we have to tell in order to find the truth? Don't deceive yourself. Tell me if it's really love that we feel.

ALMA. I love.

SAUL. Yes, but according to my rules, my vision. It was easy to imitate Mother and Father. Simply a matter of chemistry.

ALMA. But we...

SAUL. No, you and I! Never we!

ALMA. Why are you telling me all this?

SAUL. I love the way she taught me to love, as she demanded.

ALMA. It's only logical, we were a family. Who but they would teach us about love?

SAUL. What did you learn? What have you learned living through them? What happened to their love? Oh, I'm sure they were in love at one time, a moment of conviction, a fleeting moment, but then, what? We came into being?

ALMA. Hearing you talk like this makes me want to vomit!

SAUL. Say the word love and you'll feel the same nausea. Look deep into your heart and try to find it. There's nothing. Only faint ghosts among the memories.

ALMA. Where is this leading to, Saul?

SAUL. Have you ever thought about suicide?

ALMA. No, I mean, sometimes. No!

SAUL. Wasn't death always hovering over us? Wouldn't we feel alive by pretending death doesn't exist?

ALMA. Perhaps...

SAUL. If it's the beginning and not the end, like we thought, then it's the only thing viable, real, consistent.

ALMA. It would be taking a very big risk.

SAUL. But the last one! The ultimate risk! *(Embracing her tenderly.)* Alma, I'm afraid. Terribly afraid.

ALMA. Take out the pistol. It's there, in that trunk.

SAUL. Who first?

ALMA. Ladies first. Then I bet you in the other life we find Mother and Father laughing at us.

SAUL. Does it have bullets?

ALMA. It's always loaded. One never knows when it'll come in handy.

SAUL. *(Giving her the pistol.)* Take it.

ALMA. Remember, you're next.

SAUL. Shouldn't we leave a message, so no one will be blamed?

ALMA. Who could possibly be at fault?

SAUL. All right. Let's start...

ALMA. You do it. *(Giving him the pistol.)*

SAUL. Me?

ALMA. At least do me that favor.

SAUL. Which side should I shoot at?

ALMA. The right side.

SAUL. Wouldn't it be better in the heart?

ALMA. I would stain myself. And in my green dress, I'll look like the Mexican flag.

SAUL. And your last wish?

ALMA. None of my wishes ever came true! This will be more of the same.

SAUL. All right, let's do it.

ALMA. Shoot me several times.

SAUL. Merry Christmas.

ALMA. Same to you. *(Several shots are heard as Alma reacts to each discharge. Silence. Saul looks at the pistol as Alma feels her body for the wounds.)* What happened? Did the gun go off?

SAUL. You're not dead?

ALMA. Saul! There's no blood!

SAUL. My God! Then we're not dreaming!

ALMA. And you fired all the rounds! What were you planning to do? Kill only me? Egotist?

SAUL. But then, what happened? If we can't die...Oh, this is terrible!

ALMA. Oh Saul, we are a myth!

SAUL. *(Looking at the skeleton.)* We have to bring them back to life!

ALMA. We can't play God!

SAUL. But if neither life nor death is possible, what then?

ALMA. We have to find a way out!

SAUL. I can't think of anything! Our death was a marvelous ending!

ALMA. Why are you staring at Mother and Father? Let them rest in peace.

SAUL. Yes, they only left us these fleshless bones, this dusty memory.

ALMA. But we have to die! You told me we had to dignify our existence!

SAUL. *(Approaches the skeletons.)* We're less than them. They won! They're eternal, we're not! And they're the ones who screamed at us to let them live while they trampled on us every minute!

ALMA. Yes, but, I don't understand. What are you thinking of now?

SAUL. It's very simple. Take off their clothes! *(Alma looks at him perplexed.)* Don't argue with me! Take off their clothes! *(Alma, disconcerted, proceeds to undress the skeletons.)* You'll see, you'll see! We'll be happy and free! We'll give the orders around here...No one will suspect a thing! Only Alma and me! Only the two of us!

ALMA. Then you and I will remain alive?

SAUL. Not like you think. Dress up in Mother's clothes!

ALMA. What?

SAUL. *(Taking off his clothes.)* We'd better start getting used to it...Madame Venturina.

ALMA. Saul, I don't see the point of all this...

SAUL. Nicolás! From this moment on, we'll be Venturina and Nicolás! Understand? *(Saul puts on his father's tuxedo and takes hold of his cane.)* We'll be Father and Mother. The ideal couple!

ALMA. I hadn't thought of that! *(Quickly, Alma dresses in her mother's clothes.)*

SAUL. Now we can really fall in love like they did! By becoming them!

ALMA. And find that moment when they truly loved each other!

SAUL. That's what we'll have to discover at our leisure, Madame Venturina.

ALMA. Our children will be proud of us! *(Alma dresses the skeletons in the children's clothes.)*

SAUL. Saul is a fine looking lad! My spitting image, like they say!

ALMA. Alma was prettier. She had many suitors. They followed her everywhere. Besieged her. Waited on her every move, showered gifts on her. Alma was prettier.

SAUL. Put your daughter near the tree. She'll look better next to those lights.

ALMA. Alma loved to decorate the tree. It filled her with nostalgia and melancholy. I never understood why.

SAUL. We'll put Saul there...by the window.

ALMA. No! They should always be together. That way not even Christmas can separate them! Bring him here...next to Almita...next to me.

SAUL. Woman, are you mad? From now on we can't confuse them. This is the definitive game!

ALMA. Be tolerant, Nicolás. Let them do what they want to, put them to sleep in the same bed every night, let them kiss each other in front of us, so they'll trust us...

SAUL. But don't you understand?

ALMA. Our parents never did it because they were afraid to dream.

SAUL. Who are you referring to?

ALMA. *(Pointing to the skeletons.)* To their grandparents, of course!

SAUL. Then everything is understood?

ALMA. Quite clearly!

SAUL. And do you know why they committed suicide?

ALMA. Suicide? But, Nicolás, they're alive!

SAUL. After what they did to us?

ALMA. What are you trying to say?

SAUL. That this isn't a game, it's revenge! *(Saul takes the pistol.)*

ALMA. You can't do it! There are no more bullets!

SAUL. Only two destinies that must end! *(With uncontainable fury he starts hitting the skulls with the pistol butt.)*

ALMA. *(Raising her voice as though she were praying aloud.)* Alma and Saul were two healthy children. Born like the rest of us. Son of Venturina and Nicolás. They lived in a big metropolis. One day two little corpses were found in a state of decomposition. No one was alarmed. No one investigated. No museum reclaimed their bones. All we know is that they were killed and that for centuries they remained next to an artificial Christmas tree. We also know that their souls rest in a celestial court and that both changed their names for a pseudonym.

SAUL. No one will ever be able to destroy the world we gave them!

ALMA. They wanted to be forgiven. They wanted to be themselves.

SAUL. Like two rotten corpses?

ALMA. Like two who dreamed.

SAUL. There will be no more dreaming in my house! *(We hear the church bells, followed by a long silence.)*

ALMA. *(Getting on the wheelchair.)* Midnight.

SAUL. Yes. Let's go to sleep. It's been a long day. *(Kisses her on the cheek.)* At least tomorrow I don't have to work. I can sleep really late. *(Slowly moving the chair.)* What a dream! There's no doubt about it—we're old, Venturina—everything tires us now! Ah, if only we were young!

ALMA. We'd be singing another song, Nicolás.

(Sound of bells rising in intensity. The old people exit in total silence. The curtain closes, leaving us with the image of two skeletons dressed like Alma and Saul next to the Christmas tree.)

THE END

I. *The Fickle Finger of Lady Death* by the Puerto Rican Traveling Theater in New York, 1994. Oscar de la Fe Colón, Roberto Rodríguez, and Sandra Rodríguez as *La Catrina*. (Photo courtesy of the Puerto Rican Traveling Theater.)

II. *The Fickle Finger of Lady Death* by the Puerto Rican Traveling Theater in New York, 1994. Left to right: Miriam Cruz as *The Mother*, Jorge Oliver as *Juanito*, Oscar de la Fe Colón as *The Father*, and Ivonne Caro as *Josefina*. (Photo courtesy of the Puerto Rican Traveling Theater.)

III. *Profane Games* by Teatro Dallas, 1991. Cora Cardona as *Alma*. (Photo courtesy of Teatro Dallas.)

IV. *Profane Games* by Teatro Dallas, 1991. Scott Latham as *Saul* and Cora Cardona as *Alma*. (Photo courtesy of Teatro Dallas.)

V. *The Tree* by Teatro Dallas, 1993. Cora Cardona as *Luisa* and Stacy Wilson as *Marta*. (Photo by David Moynihan.)

VI.   *Homicidio Calificado (Murder With Malice)*, Instituto Nacional de Bellas Artes, 1994.   Osvaldo Gutiérrez as *David Rodríguez*, and Fernando Tolle Laphan as *The Abuelo*.   (Photo courtesy of Víctor Hugo Rascón Banda)

VII. *Homicidio Calificado (Murder With Malice),* Instituto Nacional de Bellas Artes, 1994. Alfredo Alfonso as *Rubén Sandoval* (Photo courtesy of Víctor Hugo Rascón Banda.)

VIII.   *Homicidio Calificado (Murder With Malice),* Instituto Nacional de Bellas Artes, 1994. Alejandro Tomassi as *Darrell Cain.* Alfredo Gutiérrez as *Santos Rodríguez.* (Photos courtesy of Víctor Hugo Rascón Banda.)

THE FICKLE FINGER OF LADY DEATH

by

EDUARDO RODRIGUEZ SOLIS

TRANSLATED FROM THE SPANISH

by

CARLOS MORTON

The English-language premier of THE FICKLE FINGER OF LADY DEATH took place on July 30, 1994 in New York City. It was produced by the Puerto Rican Traveling Theater and directed by Jorge Huerta.

CHARACTERS

(To be performed with five men and three women)

ACTRESS I, *Lady Death*

ACTOR I, *Father, Facundo, First man, First friend*

ACTRESS II, *Mother, Angustias, Voice, Irma*

ACTOR II, *Juanito, T.V. repairman, Bartender, Anastasio*

ACTRESS III, *Josefina, T.V. addict, Newsboy, Rosalinda*

ACTOR III, *Vendor, Admiral, Con man, Johnnie*

ACTOR IV, *Little Fling, Nosy, American, Florist*

ACTOR V, *Meliton, Second man, Second friend, Taxi driver*

THE SCENE

In and around present-day Mexico City

(Enter La Catrina or Lady Death, as pictured by the famous Mexican illustrator, José Guadalupe Posada.)

CATRINA. I know everyone in the whole world. At times you overwhelm me. But my presence here shouldn't be any cause for alarm. After all, one of these days you'll all be getting a visit from little old me. Besides, all of us have, at one time or another, taken death as a kind of joke. Why not do it for art's sake? I, La Catrina, am not the demonic adversary of mankind but rather just the opposite...a good friend, a bosom buddy you can share a laugh with. In Mexico everyone makes fun of me, with skeletons on All Souls Day, in the drawings of José Guadalupe Posada, in popular songs and ballads, with ghastly cardboard skeletons or colorful sugar skulls. They not only call me Lady Death, but all sorts of names: The Skeleton, Old Baldy, Bone Head, Marble Top, Toothless, Hardheaded, Smiley, Skinny, Shaky, the Grim Reaper, Old Goat Shanks, Our Lady of the Veil, the Pale One, the Dark One, the Sad One, the Weeper, the Stinker, the Sooty One, Our Lady of the Apocalypse. And what do we say when one of our friends is about to shuffle off his mortal coil: He's gone to "the Great Beyond, the Netherworld, the Underworld, the Great Divide, Abraham's Bosom, the Big Sleep, the Deep End, the Last Roundup." Well, call me what you wish, but when the curtain goes down, tricky little me is there to continue the morbid jokes and to tell you about the way people found death (that is, me) in hilarious or odd ways. Upon this stage we will present seven moments from beyond the grave, of which I am the principal protagonist. Only two of these scenes are bloody. But when that moment comes it will be done in jest, because the theater of the world is filled with little white lies. And so this blood will be make believe. Another of the peculiar things about this spectacle is that there will be a contest among the victims to see who can give the best rendition of a famous song I used to sing long ago. At the end of this play you will pick the winner (or loser) of the contest. Perhaps one of you will make the award in person and carry a laurel wreath to the grave of your favorite performer, for, as the saying goes: There are two things in life of which one is certain: Death and taxes. The song, by the way, goes like this:

(Singing.)

Adiós, muchachos, compañeros de mi vida...etc. And now allow me to open up my heart (if only I had one) and offer you my first little tale: "The Man Who Overdosed on a Cheese Torta." Imagine, if you will, that Juanito *(Juanito, the Bridegroom, enters and bows politely to the audience.)* and Josefina *(She enters and also greets the audience.)* are on the eve of their wedding day. Both are to be found at the bride's home with her parents.

FATHER. I'm Josefina's father.

MOTHER. I'm Josefina's mother.

LA CATRINA. They are here to take the wedding picture.

JUANITO. You know. Me all dressed up in my tuxedo, standing tall, smiling at the camera behind a velvet covered sofa where my bride is sitting, grinning from ear to ear.

JOSEFINA. I am posing innocently, my hands clutching a white bouquet.

JUANITO. I place my hand on my bride's shoulder...

LA CATRINA. The wedding photo. What we all hang up in the living room. The symbol of the Mexican family. Here they are, the future bride and groom, on the eve of that momentous date. The photo is taken and Juanito excuses himself.

MOTHER. But Juanito, you simply can't leave without having a bite to eat. Would you turn your nose up at my tasty little supper?

JUANITO. But Ma'am, I've got to be up early. Tomorrow's the wedding day. I have to wash up and put on my tuxedo.

LA CATRINA. It's important to note that Juanito's tummy is a bottomless pit. This is to say that he stuffs himself like a pig.

JUANITO. Well, let me tell you that old Goat Shanks exaggerates a wee bit. For example, I had a very light breakfast today. A small glass of orange juice, half a papaya, huevos rancheros with ham, beans, a veal cutlet, a large mug of hot chocolate, two rolls, and couple of pan dulces.

LA CATRINA. And for lunch what did you limit yourself to, dear Juanito?

JUANITO. A small shrimp cocktail, a bowl of garlic soup, a steak, a double portion of strawberry shortcake, and two cappuccinos.

LA CATRINA. And that's why I say, ladies and gentlemen, that Juanito is a bottomless pit.

JUANITO. *(To the bride's mother.)* I do appreciate the invitation, Ma'am, but really, I must get up at the crack of dawn. Because tomorrow, as you well know and have given your permission, there will be a wedding. And in this ceremony your daughter and I play very important roles.

JOSEFINA. *(To the audience.)* Afterwards we're off to Acapulco. We have our bus tickets reserved. And in the Hotel Acapoopoo there's a little room waiting for us.

FATHER. But Juanito, you're not going to insult my wife's cooking, are you?

MOTHER. I'm going to warm up some leftover paella from lunch, and there are some nice little tamales from Oaxaca, thick chocolate, some hot churros, and a nice café con leche.

JUANITO. Well, what can I say...*(To the audience.)* I'll have to find a little spot in the storeroom of my stomach. I'll have to sacrifice and prove that I'm not rude.

LA CATRINA. And the dishes start marching in. And the cries of joy uttered by Juanito prove my point. *(The actor who plays Juanito pantomimes the eating of each plate as it is served. The others urge him on.)*

MOTHER. What do you think of the paella? I hope you don't mind eating leftovers.

JUANITO. I'm speechless!

JOSEFINA. What about the tamales from Oaxaca?

JUANITO. They knock me out!

FATHER. How's the hot chocolate?

JUANITO. Breathtaking!

LA CATRINA. And what about the churros and the café con leche?

JUANITO. Why, my dear Catrina, they're to DIE FOR!

LA CATRINA. Now you know this bottomless pit, Juanito Balmaceda, who tomorrow is marrying the most beautiful girl in the neighborhood of Santa María la Ribera...

JOSEFINA. That's me...

LA CATRINA. This Juanito Balmaceda is absolutely bursting at the seams, like a Mexico City subway car during rush hour...

MOTHER. I hope you had enough to eat.

FATHER. Would you like to take some chocolate along for the road?

JOSEFINA. Some churritos in a bag?

JUANITO. No thanks. *(To the audience.)* I'm stuffed...

FATHER. Well, then, goodnight.

MOTHER. Take care.

JOSEFINA. Remember that you have to be at the church a little before eleven.

JUANITO. *(To the audience.)* It's an appointment I can't afford to miss.

LA CATRINA. The man walks out to the street. The moon is in all its splendor. At the corner of Nonoalco and Pino the man who is to get married tomorrow waits anxiously for his bus. But time goes by and he goes on waiting.

VENDOR. Hey pal, you got another half hour before the next bus comes by. Come on over where there's light. You don't want to get mugged.

LA CATRINA. Juanito approaches the light...

JUANITO. *(To the audience.)* You're not going to believe this, but I'm hungry...

LA CATRINA. What did I tell you? Juanito is a bottomless pit.

JUANITO. I'm not that bad, my dear Catrina.

VENDOR. What can I get you?

JUANITO. Gosh, I hope God doesn't strike me down...Well, make me a torta with lots of cheese and some tomato and jalapeños, of course. And a Coca-Cola, please.

VENDOR. *(As he prepares the torta.)* This cheese is super fresh...So, you're getting married to Josefina. I remember when she used to go to school with her blue uniform and white collar. How time flies. *(Gives torta to Juanito who tastes it.)* Well, how does it taste?

JUANITO. Oh, this cheese is to DIE FOR.

LA CATRINA. And the man packs in his torta and washes it down with Coca Cola. Me? I just lay low, waiting to spring into action. Juanito Balmaceda bids adieu to the torta vendor. Curiously enough, he says "goodbye" instead of "see you later." And there he is, waiting for his bus. All at once he feels a prickling sensation from head to toe. He turns pale (perhaps wanting to imitate me) and his head starts to spin.

He gasps for air...but the end is near...and it's time to take my hand.

JUANITO. *(Desperately.)* I'm done for. It's time to hang up the tennies. It's time to go beddy-by in my PJ's made of pine.

LA CATRINA. It's also time to sing the song...

JUANITO. *(Singing.)* Adiós, muchachos, compañeros de mi vida, etc.

LA CATRINA. Well, poor Juanito Balmaceda ran out of gas, crashed, broke his headlights, punched out his tires, and all because of a cheese torta with tomato and jalapeños. But luckily Lady Death came at a happy time. You even saw it yourselves, Juanito Balmaceda left this world with a smile on his lips. The moral, if there is one: You are what you eat. In this case it was the cheese that laid low our dear friend. And now, let's go on to another story: "The Proof is in the Pudding." In Mexico City, as in every city, there are cautious men who never tire themselves out, breathe fresh air, eat regular meals, and who think that they can live forever. Such is the case of the celebrated figure of Don Facundo Cabrera, an experienced agent of the Public Prosecutor's Office who is known as El Marquis. Well, this Marquis just happens to have a wife who is full of spirit, with a lust for life...

DOÑA ANGUSTIAS. *(Entering and introducing herself.)* My name is Doña Angustias. I'm the wife of Facundo Cabrera, better known as El Marquis. I'm not as young as I used to be, but my blood flows as hot as a lusty girl's. And everyone calls me Dolly.

LA CATRINA. As I was saying, El Marquis, whose wife is full of the devil with a lust for life, is a man completely wedded to his job, with little time for Dolly.

DON FACUNDO. *(Entering, mumbling.)* An amazing case. Absolutely unbelievable. It turns out that a young man named Rodolfo Valentino Hernández was found in his apartment flat on his back with his breath reeking of garlic and onions. The autopsy turned up the fact that the young man was accidentally poisoned. He died in place of a dog. The dog goes on barking his head off and driving everyone crazy, while Rudolfo Valentino Hernández is now making his own racket on a harp, as an accompanist to St. Peter.

LA CATRINA. And how did all this come about, Mr. Marquis?

DOÑA ANGUSTIAS. What a bore...

DON FACUNDO. The young man arrived home at one thirty-five in the morning and exactly twenty feet to the east of his car he happened upon an enormous bone filled with fresh bone marrow. He recalled that during his childhood his grandmother made a lively broth with bones she bought from a local butcher. He stretched out his hand, carefully picked up the bone and entered his building. As he climbed the steps leading to his apartment he decided to revive the old family custom and stopped off at a neighbor's to borrow a bit of garlic and onion. Once inside his kitchen he lit the stove and put on a big pot of water. He popped in the bone and when the mess came to a boil he seasoned it to taste and served himself a big bowl garnished with onions and garlic. He waited until it cooled and then gobbled it up. Five minutes later he was laid out flat on the floor.

LA CATRINA. And why do you claim he was poisoned by accident?

DOÑA ANGUSTIAS. What a bore.

DON FACUNDO. Because according to the investigation this bone was planted there for the expressed purpose of putting a barking dog out of commission. Doña Gertrudes Sánchez confessed to having prepared the poisoned bone that killed our friend. The dog, according to witnesses, continues driving everyone in the neighborhood crazy.

DOÑA ANGUSTIAS. Are you back already, Facundo dear? How are things at the Public Prosecutor's Office? Anything new?

DON FACUNDO. What news should there be? Dead people and more dead people. The usual.

DOÑA ANGUSTIAS. How do you like my new dress?

DON FACUNDO. One of them leaps from a fifth story window, and another throws himself in front of a subway train.

DOÑA ANGUSTIAS. It's a red dress with blue flowers.

DON FACUNDO. This afternoon I have to go and pick up some drunk who knocked himself out on a lamp post.

DOÑA ANGUSTIAS. Red and blue looks good on me.

LA CATRINA. That's how it goes, day after day. The man doesn't look after his wife. First comes work, then more work, followed by still more work. That's why the woman must occupy herself with little things. And these little things become little flings that make her happy. Because that little fling is aglow with youth and shares her lust for life.

LITTLE FLING. *(Entering as though he were a great dancer from a 1930s musical film.)* The little thing. Yes, sir. The Little Fling. Here you find joy with your little boy. Brush the old man aside and let me take you for a ride.

DOÑA ANGUSTIAS. Will you be my Little Fling?

LITTLE FLING. Your wish is my command.

DOÑA ANGUSTIAS. Then fling your thing!

LA CATRINA. The woman whose husband pays no attention to her must occupy herself with little flings. But sooner or later things must come to a head.

LITTLE FLING. I'm tired of all this pussy-footing, playing hide-and-go-seek in hidden corners, meeting in flop houses and dark bars. I want to make love to you in your house, here on this chaise longue!

LA CATRINA. Point of clarification. The chaise longue is most conducive to paramours. It's a sofa in the form of a bed, generally upholstered in gold velvet, decorated with carved wood and gilt. It's Cupid's Love Nest, a convenient receptacle for torrid trysts.

DOÑA ANGUSTIAS. But, how can we do this?

LITTLE FLING. We've got to wipe him off the map.

DOÑA ANGUSTIAS. But how can one rub out a Public Prosecutor?

LITTLE FLING. Easy as pie. We have to do it. We must be firm. We must gird our loins!

DOÑA ANGUSTIAS. Where are you going?

LITTLE FLING. To buy some pinole. I'll explain later.

DOÑA ANGUSTIAS. Oh, where will all this passion take us?

LA CATRINA. The answer is quite simple. The solution to the lovebird's problem is in the pudding.

DON FACUNDO. What's there to eat today? What did you make?

DOÑA ANGUSTIAS. A shrimp broth, white rice and black beans, although some might call it "a mixed marriage," and a nice little steak.

DON FACUNDO. What's for dessert?

DOÑA ANGUSTIAS. For dessert? Ah...

LA CATRINA. *(Whispering to Doña.)* A surprise.

DOÑA ANGUSTIAS. Oh, it's a surprise.

LA CATRINA. The man eats his dinner and reads the crime reports in the newspaper to keep up with the activities of his colleagues.

LITTLE FLING. *(Entering at a run.)* Here is the pinole pudding.

DOÑA ANGUSTIAS. What am I supposed to do with it?

LA CATRINA. Pour it into a bowl and cover it with a napkin. Then shut all the windows so the pinole doesn't blow away.

DON FACUNDO. What a delicious meal. Now for a nice dessert and afterwards an expresso and a good cigar.

DOÑA ANGUSTIAS. Here you are, your Honor.

LA CATRINA. Don Facundo is about to take a firm stand. He's about to find some hard luck.

DON FACUNDO. I don't think I feel like dessert after all.

DOÑA ANGUSTIAS. Eat your dessert like a good boy.

DON FACUNDO. No.

DOÑA ANGUSTIAS. Yes.

DON FACUNDO. All right, if you insist.

DOÑA ANGUSTIAS. Pinole pudding from Puebla, made with the very best cinnamon.

DON FACUNDO. Hmmm...

DOÑA ANGUSTIAS. *(To Lady Death.)* What am I supposed to do now?

LA CATRINA. Go to the refrigerator and get an ice cube.

DOÑA ANGUSTIAS. What? An ice cube?

LA CATRINA. An ice cube.

LITTLE FLING. What's the idea?

LA CATRINA. Ice, on contact with the skin, produces a reaction, doesn't it?

LITTLE FLING. Well, so what?

LA CATRINA. The ice comes sliding down the old man's spine causing a terrible short circuit. The pinole powder gets stuck in his throat causing him to suffocate.

LITTLE FLING. Almost like snorting...poison.

DOÑA ANGUSTIAS. Here's the ice cube.

LA CATRINA. Well, now you stalk him like a vamp, hiding, of course, the ice, and get closer and closer to Don Facundo Cabrera, alias El Marquis.

DON FACUNDO. What's the matter with you?

DOÑA ANGUSTIAS. Round and round I go and where I stop nobody knows. But in a minute your lights will dim and your soul will fly out of your mouth!

LA CATRINA. Steady, Angustias. Hold on, Facundo. Now, Angustias, let the ice cube fall and let it slide down Facundo's spine! *(Angustias drops the ice down his back; the reaction causes him to choke on the pinole.)*

DON FACUNDO. They revoked my driver's license, tore up my I.D. card, La Catrina is making eyes at me, and my soul is flying out of my mouth!

LA CATRINA. Give me your hand, it's time for you to sing your song.

DON FACUNDO. *(Sings.)* Adiós, muchachos, compañeros de mi vida, etc.

LA CATRINA. If Don Facundo hadn't deserved the nickname of El Marquis, and if he'd been good enough to caress his wife once in a while, things might have turned out differently. But it's obvious that men will be men and women were made to suffer. Isn't that so, dear Angustias? *(But by this time Angustias and her little fling are deeply involved.)* Let us tune in to the times we live by turning on the television. The boob tube persuades us to buy this and do that. T.V. is like a cigarette habit, it's hard to stop cold. It's our daily six pack. Our next story: "The Woman Who Died Trying to be a Television Repair Person."

(Enter Meliton, a working class stiff, putting on his jacket. His wife, a notorious T.V. addict, follows him.)

MELITON. Well, I'm off to work, let's see if you can keep your promise.

T.V. ADDICT. Of course, Meliton, this time I will keep my promise.

MELITON. Oh, my dear couch potato, you can't tear yourself away from the tube. Just look at this house. That mountain of dirty dishes in the sink. This floor.

T.V. ADDICT. You go to work and let me take care of my wifely chores. *(To the audience.)* That's what he thinks. *(To Meliton.)* The time has come for me to straighten up. From now on I'll be a good girl. *(She winks at the audience.)*

MELITON. Your soul is a soap opera. Your middle initials should be T.V.

T.V. ADDICT. Alicia T.V. Fernández, at your service.

MELITON. You can't live without those T.V. serials. Just look at those cockroaches and the mouse poking its head out there. And this floor that's dirtier than the soul of the world's worst sinner.

T.V. ADDICT. Keep your nose out of my business. It's my dirt. And the cockroaches and rats are my little friends who keep me company. *(To the audience.)* Since my husband is never home I have to find some way to occupy my time. With T.V. I find an all powerful God who offers me advice. What to eat, what to buy, what opinions to have regarding world affairs, the songs I should sing, and what movies to enjoy. Television is also like a mirror where I watch myself acting out the greatest, most exciting soap operas.

MELITON. Well, I'm off. It's time to catch the subway to the factory and get to the riveting job of riveting. We have to turn out lots of cars so that middle-class people can race across town at full speed...or drive up to some lonely place with a floozy in search of the intimacy we can't get from our own wives, who, after all, are the real owners of our paychecks and make us our daily bread. Yesterday I drove 786 rivets. Today I've got to break 800. It's the only way I can make an extra two hundred pesos.

T.V. ADDICT. Well, then, get to it, dear husband, what are you waiting for?

MELITON. O.K., catch you later, honey bunch. Don't get too carried away with the T.V..

T.V. ADDICT. Don't worry. *(To audience.)* That's what he thinks.

MELITON. Tell your cockroaches and mice I said good-bye.

T.V. ADDICT. *(To audience.)* It's terrible! No one understands my suffering. But in the final analysis I wear the skirts in this family. Nobody better bad mouth or lay a hand on my cockroaches and mice, nobody! They're my little pets, all mine!

VOICE (OFF). Teevee Addict!

T.V. ADDICT. *(To the audience.)* It's my neighbor, Doña Chonita, who lives in Number 83. Excuse me a minute, I'll be right back. Yes, Doña Chonitaaaaaaa.

VOICE. Say, what finally happened to Lupita yesterday? I didn't get a chance to watch the show.

T.V. ADDICT. They found out that that awful Armando was going with two women behind her back, and so Lupita went to see her lawyer to start the divorce proceedings. And you'll never guess what happened next?

VOICE. I have no idea!

T.V. ADDICT. Well that lawyer made indecent proposals to her and they went off for a little stroll.

VOICE. How horrible! What people will do.

T.V. ADDICT. Would you believe it?

VOICE. That soap opera is the hottest thing around.

T.V. ADDICT. Of the 43 soaps on T.V., I think it's the very best.

VOICE. Do you really think it's better than the one on Channel 76?

T.V. ADDICT. Of course. What happens to Lupita could happen to anyone of us.

VOICE. Well, I don't agree with you.

T.V. ADDICT. You have a right to your own opinion.

VOICE. Oh, no! Something's burning! I think it's the beans.

T.V. ADDICT. *(To audience.)* Hmph, trying to tell me which is the best soap opera. That'll be the day. I know them all by heart. *(To her pets.)* Isn't that so, my dear little cockroaches, my darling mice. *(Beat.)* Oh, my goodness, the bells for Mass are ringing, it's time for *Laughter, Smiles and Romances.* Where's my T.V. set? Where's my black and white Admiral? *(Enter the black and white Admiral.)*

ADMIRAL. Here I am. *(Giving a military salute.)* Present and accounted for, Chief! Ready to begin the daily battle.

T.V. ADDICT. My dear Admiral, have you been working too much? You don't look so hot.

ADMIRAL. Well, that's what we're here for. We're created to serve society and transmit social values. So we have to work to the death. It's our fate. You just give the orders, Madam.

T.V. ADDICT. Well then, I'll just have to plug you in because *Laughter, Smiles and Romance* is about to start.

ADMIRAL. I feel my circuits abuzz with cultural energy born in the womb of the television networks...I greet you Fabulous Mexican Family, from the heart of Make-Sick-O-City. I invite you to sit down and hear how it's time to go to the Pérez Department Store to purchase that much-needed bedroom suite which is on sale for the incredibly low price of only thirty thousand pesos. I also must say, Fabulous Mexican Family, that tonight you must go eat hamburgers at the nearest fast food outlet where for only forty-four pesos and ninety cents you can dine on a Monsterburger made from freshly killed steer meat, with a slice of American cheese. Also, Fabulous Mexican Family I want to say that there is a Mustang automobile in your future, waiting for you, so that you can stop riding the Metro. Subway rides are for the common people. And you, Fabulous Mexican Family, are not common but quite the contrary. Ding-Dong-Ding. XYZ, Channel 41, the fun channel, the only channel. Tan-tara-tan-ta-ta-ta! Another chapter of *Laughter, Smiles and Romance*, number 836 of the most widely acclaimed series on Mexican television. An extraordinary soap opera, fantastic, full of surprises, incredible, unbelievable...*(The Admiral starts making strange noises.)*

T.V. ADDICT. Admiral, old friend, what's wrong? What's happening to you?

ADMIRAL. My heart...I mean...my picture tube!

T.V. ADDICT. You can't possibly die right now! Just when I need you the most! You can't betray me now. How rude!

ADMIRAL. It's just that...my bulbs are burning out...my time has come...I want my mommy!

T.V. ADDICT. *(To audience.)* Is there a doctor in the house? I mean, is there a T.V. repairman in the house? Please, have pity. Is there a repairman out there? *(Enter a T.V. repairman.)*

REPAIRMAN. What's all this racket? Where's the disaster? Where's the fire? Show me the dead and injured.

T.V. ADDICT. Are you a T.V. repairman?

REPAIRMAN. Black and white and color...here's my license.

T.V. ADDICT. Hurry, he's tuning out...I mean, my favorite program's about to start. Quick, bring him back to life!

REPAIRMAN. All right, Ma'am, stand behind me so I can get to work. Don't get too close, there could be some high voltage here. You wouldn't want to get shocked. *(The repairman examines the set. The Admiral T.V. is failing fast, giving off strange noises.)* It's beyond help. You have to change the picture tube. It'll run you about five thousand pesos. You're the boss, Ma'am, let me know if I can put a new one in.

T.V. ADDICT. Five thousand pesos! That's highway robbery. Get out of here you dirty rotten good-for-nothing crook! *(The repairman exits running.)*

VOICE (OFF). TEEVEE addict! The program started! Don't miss it!

T.V. ADDICT. My dear Admiral, don't do this to me. Don't let me down!

REPAIRMAN. *(Entering again.)* Look, I forgot to charge you for the house call. That'll be fifty pesos. *(T.V. addict doesn't hear him. She is on her knees in front of the T.V. set. The repairman understands this little drama, which our fabulous Mexican family lives.)* Well, I'm not leaving here with empty hands. I'll take this bottle of milk and sack of rolls in exchange for my services. *(Exits.)*

T.V. ADDICT. I'll bring you back to life.

ADMIRAL. *(Trying to warn her as she inserts her hands in the "set.")* No, no, not from behind! There are high voltage wires there! It'll be the death of you!

T.V. ADDICT. *(Acting like she has just been electrocuted.)* Wow! I just won a ticket to Paradise. I've punched the old time clock! I busted my bulbs.

LA CATRINA. *(Entering.)* T.V. is a habit you just can't kick. A double edged sword. The addict takes me by the hand and starts to exit this world. She shoots past the stars and the infinite galaxies. She passes close to the communications satellites, fading into the darkness of outer space, singing...

T.V. ADDICT. *(Singing!)* Adiós, muchachos, compañeros de mi vida, etc.

LA CATRINA. Like a guided missile, the T.V. addict was propelled from the planet. Many others exit this galaxy in the same way. The human missiles streak through space, spinning around, often missing their mark. One wants to go one way, and ends up in another spot by sheer coincidence. The stories are full of surprise endings, often sinister. Blood shoots out as a matter of course. But remember that this blood, like everything else in the theater of the world, is stage blood, a simple illusion, like my own transparent soul, like my own little heart that is food for maggots. All stories have their local color. And the one that follows is like the dusk, gray, like the color of the earth's soul. It is a tale of infinite derision, of chance happenings. The title: "Hard Rocks in the Land of Hard Knocks."

FIRST MAN. Listen, compadre, I don't give a hoot what you say or think.

SECOND MAN. Compadre, I asked you loud and clear if you wouldn't mind buying another round of beers.

FIRST MAN. Sure, that's what I said, compadre, but you didn't let me finish.

SECOND MAN. What were you going to add, compadre?

FIRST MAN. That I'd buy another round of beers, but that I don't have the money.

SECOND MAN. So what am I going to say to my old lady when I show up at the house without a penny in my pocket?

FIRST MAN. Just say: Look, my pockets are empty, but my belly's full of beer!

SECOND MAN. Is that the way to treat your compadre?

FIRST MAN. You don't like it?

SECOND MAN. No, I don't!

FIRST MAN. You don't scare me!

SECOND MAN. Well, let's get it on!

LA CATRINA. And that's how the blood letting starts. The argument begins over nothing and before you know it's all blown out of proportion. The two friends, who could be any one of us, suddenly revert back to the days of the cave men. And that's when I get involved. Although my job is to punch out somebody's lights, it's hard to choose. Destiny and luck figure into these matters. Often a third party (it could be you or you or you) steps in and takes my hand for a journey to the great beyond. *(During this speech the two combatants continue their argument.)*

NOSY. *(Enter a nosy meddler.)* I'm Eduardito, the nosy meddler. And you know what? *(Talking to the audience.)* Just a little while ago I almost got my head broken. I was standing on the corner of Londres and Génova watching the gringas walking by. In back of me, sitting on the sidewalk, was one of those beggar women they call the India María. Some say she's hired by radicals to embarrass the government because no one really needs to beg in our country. India María is carrying a tiny baby girl in her arms whose cheeks are grimy and whose little arms are as thin as sticks—just like La Catrina. India María was pleading for a handout when up comes this snooty, well-dressed matron who ordered her off the street. I, Eduardito, got really upset. I jumped into the conversation and told the old goat where to get off. The snooty matron asked a cop on the corner for help and the copper said to me: "You get out of here or I'll break this club over your head." Well, I took off on the double with my tail between my legs.

LA CATRINA. Friends like these are a dime a dozen. They're the ones who cause all the problems. They're like the fleas we pick up at movie houses in working-class neighborhoods. But let's get back to the torrid dialogue of our two vulgar friends.

FIRST MAN. Well, listen here, compadre, it's tit for tat. Whatever you say about me goes double for you.

SECOND MAN. Well, if you want to rumble, old buddy, we can meet at dawn tomorrow with our seconds in Chapultepec Park. You choose the weapons.

FIRST MAN. But are you ready to kiss the world good-bye, old buddy?

SECOND MAN. Well, look here, old buddy, if you're ready, we'll duke it out right now.

FIRST MAN. Well, let's get it on, then.

SECOND MAN. Just remember, no hitting below the belt!

FIRST MAN. I suppose we're going to fight for the Featherweight Championship of the World!

NOSY. A dog's bark is louder than its bite. They make a lot of noise, but in the end it's all hot air.

FIRST MAN. Hey, two's company, and three's a crowd.

NOSY. They're scared to death of La Catrina, Old Goat Shanks.

FIRST MAN. All right, old buddy, get it on! Don't pay attention to this nosy ass!

SECOND MAN. Don't call me a nosy ass!

LA CATRINA. The fight starts. In this cooornerrrrrr, weighing in at 130 pounds, his belly full of cheap beeeeerrrrr, old buddy Pancracio, originally from Michoacán, and now resiiiidiiing in Mexico City where he works as a construction worker. In the other cooooornerrrrr, at 150 pounds, his belly also full of cheap beeeeerrrr, from Tacubaya, Tiburcio, the Tiger of Santa Julia! *(The fight begins. The two men put their fists up and look for an opening to strike the other.)*

NOSY. Hit him! Give it to him! You got him. Knock him dead!

LA CATRINA. One gets knocked to the ground by the other. After a few tumbles he has swallowed enough dirt. He picks up a large gray rock as big as a baseball...

SECOND MAN. No, old buddy, that's not fair. It's against Boxing Commission Rules.

FIRST MAN. To hell with the rules!

NOSY. Break his head like a piñata! Teach him to be a big mouth! Kill the bum!

LA CATRINA. Like a baseball pitcher in the big leagues, like the extraordinary Fernando Valenzuela, the first man winds up and throws the gray rock as though it were a deadly missile. The second man easily ducks and gives his old buddy the finger. The rock goes on its way hitting a lamp post and bouncing off at a thirty-three degree angle east. Next it ricochets off the front of a local store called "Odds and Ends" and goes on at an angle of twelve degrees west. A passing delivery truck carrying Pepsis and Fantas slams the rock back with extra force, towards the south...and it's final destination. *(The rock hits Nosy from behind and kills him.)*

NOSY. They've turned me into a doormat. I'm down for the count. I'm signed, sealed and delivered. I'm all wrapped up and ready to go. It's time to strum the harp.

LA CATRINA. The two buddies run inside the "Glories of Hercules," a famous dive in these mean streets. The three or four curious onlookers who pass by feign ignorance and go on their way. Extending my hand I take to hell, purgatory or heaven this busybody Eduardito whose blood flows from his broken head.

NOSY. *(Sings.)* Adiós, muchachos, compañeros de mi vida, etc.

LA CATRINA. I'd like to mention that there, in the sixth row, sits a gentleman who can't keep his eyes off me. Perhaps he's fallen for my figure or my unforgettable profile. I don't know. But he's staring so hard that, if I were really alive, I would be blushing from top to bottom. I wonder what he's thinking. Perhaps he enjoys walking among the gravestones in the cemetery where friends, once fat but now as skinny as me, sleep in eternal bliss. That reminds me of a story about a woman who decided to become as thin as yours truly. I call this story: "The Woman Who Died Wanting a Slim Figure."

CON MAN. *(Entering with the American.)* Damn, we can't even draw flies today. This Weight Watchers business is for the birds.

AMERICAN. *(With no accent.)* Hold your horses. You've got to give this scam a try.

CON MAN. But I'm practically starving to death.

AMERICAN. Just hang on a little longer.

CON MAN. I think we're going to end up flat broke.

AMERICAN. Don't worry.

CON MAN. Just look at me. I'm practically skin and bones.

AMERICAN. Calm down. There's plenty of fat suckers around. *(Irma the Gross enters. The American puts on some dark glasses and the Con Man runs off stage.)*

IRMA. Excuse me, sir...

AMERICAN. *(With an accent.)* Yes Ma'am, what can I do for you?

IRMA. You know, yesterday I cut out this ad that says, "put yourself under the care of the Weight Watchers Institute and lose weight. With a little patience, discipline and complete confidence you too can have a fantastic figure." And I do *(Timidly.)* want a nice figure. But what worries me is a news item from the evening newspaper. It says, "The fat Ortigoza girls died of a crash diet" and later on it mentions they were members of the Weight Watchers Institute.

AMERICAN. Look here, Ma'am. You know full well that when you buy a car, for instance, you run the risk that it has a factory defect. That's one of life's breaks. Man has not perfected all his inventions. But those corpulent Ortigoza girls were beyond help. By day they took the treatment, but by night they packed it in at Fat Fanny's Bar and Grill. Now, that's what caused those two chubs to short circuit.

IRMA. *(Determinedly.)* I'm willing to put everything on the line. I'll pay any price to get a slim figure like those girls in American fashion magazines.

CON MAN. *(Enters walking on his knees.)* Praise God! Praise American know-how! Praise American technology. *(He rises and begins talking to the audience.)* It's a miracle! A few days ago they called me Porky Pig. But today I am as thin as an eel. Now for sure I'll snare a movie or T.V. contract. *(Down on his knees.)* That's why I'm here, to give thanks to the Weight Watcher's Institute for saving me from disaster.

IRMA. *(To the American.)* Golly, what a miracle! What a wonderful figure!

AMERICAN. Sir, please get up. No need to make a spectacle of yourself. Our technique is applied with the utmost precision, but will power plays a big part.

IRMA. *(To audience.)* This is extraordinary! I must be in Heaven, a Paradise of skinny souls!

CON MAN. Well, I'm off! Me and my supersonic shape, my space-age slimness. No one will call me Porky Pig anymore. From now on I'll be as slim and fit as an arrow. *(Exits.)*

AMERICAN. Look here, Ma'am. I want to warn you that your case is not so simple. I see that your particular anatomy may have its wrinkles. Did you remember to bring the photographs of yourself in the buff with view from top, bottom, behind and full front?

IRMA. *(Shyly.)* Here they are. I trust you'll be discreet about this?

AMERICAN. *(With anger.)* Madam, we are a respectable institution with a prestigious track record to uphold.

IRMA. It's just that I thought...

AMERICAN. Don't you worry about a thing. Let's see, stand over there, and let me study you with this special telescope. *(Irma the Gross poses like a professional model as the American examines her through the telescope.)* Madam, in your case I'd suggest our treatment number 636.

IRMA. 636?

AMERICAN. 636. This crash diet is one of our most effective. But I must warn you, it is hair-raising, and risky.

IRMA. Hair-raising? *(To the audience.)* Oh brother, I'm scared stiff!

AMERICAN. This is the greatest Weight Watchers treatment. And to give you confidence in Method 636 I have to tell you that President Bill Clinton himself went through it before he declared his candidacy to the presidency. I must warn you, however, that in the course of the treatment you will feel as though you are about to die. But Bill had confidence in us, and later, thanks to our wisdom and his will power, managed to come out with a fairly passable figure. This helped him get elected to the highest office in the land. Naturally, he had to stop stuffing himself at McDonald's...my Lord, how he loves junk food! Bill Clinton is not the only person who made it thanks to Method 636 of the Weight Watcher's Institute. For example, let me see...*(Pauses to consider, as if trying to remember.)* Oh yes, do you remember the MGM Lion? *(Roars.)* The lion you saw roaring at the beginning of every MGM movie wasn't really a lion at all, but a lioness with a wig. She was an absolute sow. Well, this MGM Lioness made a fortune in the movies and even became known on other planets. Her popularity was so great that sailors on the high seas tattooed her profile on their biceps. After a time, she went into decline. Her manager and agent looked for other ways to exploit her talents. Her second great opportunity came at last and required that she take off so much weight as to be nothing but skin and bones. They brought her to us, the famous Weight Watcher's Institute, and upon examining the prodigious anatomy of the fat MGM Lioness we recommended Method 636. Naturally, we warned her that she would feel like dropping dead, but she would have to show the stuff she was made of. And it wasn't easy. The MGM Lioness took to her bed twice during the treatment and we almost lost her. But she forged ahead with tenacity. And she triumphed, and beat the odds. She became the skinniest lioness in existence and a star once again. Her artistic talents took her to the pinnacle. Do you know who I'm talking about?

IRMA. No, I don't. I haven't the slightest idea.

AMERICAN. *(Announcing, like a circus ringmaster.)* I am talking about the extraordinary, incomparable, the one and only Pink Panther!

IRMA. The Pink Panther?

AMERICAN. The Pink Panther.

IRMA. Well, if President Clinton and the Pink Panther did it, why can't I?

AMERICAN. Well then, Ma'am, here's your instructions. Now, I'll need a cashier's check or cash.

IRMA. There you are.

AMERICAN. But I must warn you, it's a hard row to hoe. You'll feel as though you're on the brink of death, but you must go through with it. You'll feel that the world is coming to an end, but you must grit your teeth and go full speed ahead.

IRMA. Yes, I will go through with it, even if it kills me. It's the only way.

AMERICAN. Wait a minute, don't go. I've got to take your picture.

IRMA. My picture? I don't understand.

AMERICAN. The "before picture."

IRMA. The "before" picture?

AMERICAN. Because when the treatment is over...*(To the audience.)* If she makes it to the end. *(To Irma.)* Then we take the "after" shot. You know, to be included in our famous "Before and After" file. So you'll be famous...

IRMA. Yes, of course. *(He takes her picture. Irma, ecstatic, speaks to the audience.)* That skeleton wandering over there will never get me. My fate will be like that of President Clinton and the MGM Lioness. *(Exit.)*

AMERICAN. *(Without accent.)* Mission accomplished. Service is the name of the game. *(Exit.)*

LA CATRINA. Three weeks later Irma the Gross kicked the bucket and made quite a splash in the newspaper.

IRMA. *(Entering and singing her song.)* Adiós, muchachos, compañeros de mi vide, etc.

LA CATRINA. A little advice. Don't put everything on the line to get a perfect figure. After all, we all end up in the cemetery where everyone looks the same. Skinny as the legs of a stork, as fragile and crumbly as autumn leaves. So Irma the Gross took a long walk straight to infinity. And when she was almost there she ran into the prototype of one of those men who walks from bar to bar with the hope of finding the answer to all his questions in drink. Here comes our hero. His story is called: "The Man Who Drowned a Double Death." *(Enter Johnnie Walker.)*

JOHNNIE. Johnnie Walker is my name because I am a non-stop boozer who tramps from bar to bar. I'm always high and ready to guzzle down the drinks they place in front of me. I don't even know how old I am, and count my days by the number of bars I visit.

BARTENDER. *(Entering and addressing audience.)* I'm the one who serves the drinks in all the bars of the world. I'm practically part-owner because, if you're not careful, I'll serve you a drink that will knock you for a loop. That's why I wear black, in keeping with the decor of my office. And I'm here to tell you that this young man named Johnnie Walker, even though you see him in the flesh, is no longer of the living. He went away with La Catrina to the land of no return. He has come back from the grave to teach us a lesson and to give us his rendition of what caused him to shuffle off his mortal coil in the midst of a torrential downpour. It was the month of September in Mexico City, during the rainy season, when the city looks more like Venice with all the flooding going on. The streets were filled with mud and what was left of Johnny's shoes was worn in tramping from bar to bar. It was morning, when the sun began to warm your back, and

Johnnie Walker's throat yearned for Dionysis' delirium. He staggered out of his little corrugated tin lean-to where he had spent the night on the floor, on the tatters of an old mattress. He stretched his arms and yawned, as if to say good morning to his usual hangover. Ah, it was time for a hair of the dog.

FIRST FRIEND. *(Entering with second friend.)* Look, compadre, the entire city looks like Venice. These storms are going to be the death of us.

SECOND FRIEND. Several neighborhoods have already been evacuated. The people are heading for the hills. Maybe God is punishing us.

FIRST FRIEND. The government sure doesn't help.

SECOND FRIEND. But it looks like our own neighborhood of Busted Flats will weather the storm.

FIRST FRIEND. Look here, compadre, some Red Cross volunteers. They're putting up a sign. Let's go see.

SECOND FRIEND. It's looks like the jinx is up. *(The two friends move to the other side of the stage. Meanwhile Johnny Walker goes on saying good morning to the world.)*

FIRST FRIEND. "Notice. More rain is predicted for today. According to the latest weather reports, the downpour will be concentrated in this area. We strongly advise all residents to leave the area. Please proceed at once to the top of Chiquihuite Hill. This is a state of emergency."

SECOND FRIEND. I have a cart that'll hold us both. Let's load up all our belongings.

FIRST FRIEND. Thanks, I'll take you up on that!

SECOND FRIEND. This is terrible. We're in for it now!

FIRST FRIEND. Old Goat Shanks is hot on our heels.

BARTENDER. I'd like to mention that my establishment—in which La Catrina is a partner—has always been and always will be above the water line. Allow me to indulge in a bit of self promotion by saying that when you have the urge to tie one on I am here to serve you in the Viceroy's Lookout. There, in between drinks, you've got a fine view of the entire city. My prices are right and within reach of everyone's budget. But getting back to our story, let me say that even though Johnny Walker knew how to read and write, he didn't notice the signs posted around Busted Flats because he was suffering from a tremendous hangover that morning.

JOHNNIE. Ah, this is the life! Nothing like a bit of fresh air. A nice morning to take a run up to the Viceroy's Lookout.

BARTENDER. So Johnnie Walker staggered toward my place of business. He walked along, only half-noticing the havoc that the torrential rains had wrecked. But his mind could only think of his first drink of the day. What's happening, Johnnie, aren't you afraid of getting rained out?

JOHNNIE. The only rain I'm interested in is the rain of Bacchus.

BARTENDER. What do you mean, the rain of Bacchus?

JOHNNIE. It's the only liquid that matters.

BARTENDER. Well you know, the whole city is beginning to look like Venice.

JOHNNIE. If only the canals were filled with booze! I think I could drink my way down the boulevards.

BARTENDER. Be careful. Haven't you read the signs?

JOHNNIE. Of course I've read the signs. I know them by heart. Why do you ask?

BARTENDER. You don't understand. .

JOHNNIE. I could give you lessons.

BARTENDER. But the signs say...

JOHNNIE. I know the signs by heart: "We reserve the right to refuse service to anyone including minors, women, children and uniformed personnel." And I don't fit into any of those categories. So put that in your pipe and smoke it!

BARTENDER. Look. Let's just talk about something else.

JOHNNIE. That's the "spirit". Let's get to it. Serve me a Johnnie Walker special...make it a triple!

BARTENDER. *(As he serves Johnnie.)* The man was totally out of it. He was living in an alcoholic Garden of Eden. And so I poured. The sky darkened and the rain came down. The last inhabitants of Busted Flats reached the top of Chiquihuite Hill and safety. Hours later, Johnnie Walker sang his farewell song.

JOHNNIE. *(Singing.)* Adiós, muchachos, compañeros de mi vida, etc.

NEWSBOY. *(Calling out like a newsboy.)* Extra! Extra! Read all about it. Busted Flats wiped off the map! They abandoned their homes and made a mad dash to Chiquihuite Hill! Only one dead! They say his name was Johnnie Walker and death caught him flat footed. Extra. Extra. His name was Johnnie Walker and he got soaked to the gills.

LA CATRINA.   As the torrential rains fell our friend Johnnie Walker staggered out of the Viceroy's Lookout with his belly full of booze. He sloshed to his shack with the water already waist high, walked in and curled up on his mattress. The dream he had was quite a dilly.

JOHNNIE.   *(Entering, perfectly sober, talking to the audience.)* My dream was out of this world. I was swimming in a huge pool full of boys and girls. I was floating on my back and paddling around the crystal waters. *(He exits paddling the backstroke.)*

LA CATRINA.   That's how they found him later, floating belly up. But with a happy grin on his face. The moral? The Viceroy's Lookout leads to a fall? When it rains it pours? Or better yet, "Be sure to read the handwriting on the wall." Flowers. Flowers for Johnnie Walker and for the six other victims of our little spectacle. Flowers also for the last victim of the night. But for him, appropriately, a bundle of blossoms, because his scene is filled with bouquets: "The Man Who Died Among the Flowers."

TAXI DRIVER.   I salute you who have gathered to peer through the enchanted looking glass of the stage. My scene is number seven. And seven is a magical number. Like all the others who played the game of death tonight, I am merely an actor who paints his face and fills his head with lines written by a mad poet. I have also disguised my shape with a lovely lie known as the costume because we actors are fond of masquerades. It is my turn to be the hero. And soon I will die before your eyes. But my death, just like all the other deaths experienced by my costumed colleagues, is a circus act, where fate takes center stage. That's how the Fickle Finger of Lady Death works.

FLORIST.   Saint Valentine's Day. Lover's Day. Day of friendship, day of hugs and kisses. The day of sweet nothings and serenades. Hearts falling out of rhythm in the workaday world. Sudden shivers starting at the tip of the toes and extending to the scalp. Love and more love. Love for you and love for me. Saint Valentine's Day, day of lovers.

TAXI DRIVER.   How are you doing, Don Gonzalo?   Shall we start the deliveries?

FLORIST.   Today all the flowers in the gardens and nurseries have been mowed down or plucked. But the shears of Divine Justice are swift. The stems and bodies of daisies, roses and lilies have been swiftly severed.

TAXI DRIVER.   Say, Don Gonzalo, is it true that flowers can actually feel, only they can't complain?

FLORIST.   Of course, my dear Taxi Driver. Scientists have proved this to be a fact. But Justice sits on the sidelines with her arms crossed, letting us murder the flowers. We do exactly that. We choke the life out of those beautiful beings.

TAXI DRIVER.   Then what are we selling? What are we really offering to all those sweethearts?

FLORIST. When we sell a bouquet we're actually marketing a tiny community of innocent beings who were murdered. And the sale must be a swift one because dying flowers, like men, lose their color and start to stink.

TAXI DRIVER. When flowers are no longer of any use, when they dry up, is it like throwing away their shells?

FLORIST. That's right. When we're done with them we toss them in the trash and throw away their shells.

TAXI DRIVER. How sad. It almost makes me want to cry.

FLORIST. Let's talk about other things. How's the taxi business? What's it like driving a hack?

TAXI DRIVER. The problem is that people don't have any money. That means taxi drivers are hurting. If you want an idea of what my work was like today, I started at seven in the morning. I took a lady to the hospital. It seems that her little daughter had an accident. Later on, I took an old man to the marketplace to sell chickens. After that I had a flat. And would you believe—I didn't have a jack.

FLORIST. Yes, but Valentine's Day has arrived and today you're going to make a bundle.

TAXI DRIVER. Well, let's get to work. Where do we start?

FLORIST. There are three floral arrangements and four bouquets. The addresses are clearly marked on the cards. So, let's get going, my boy!

TAXI DRIVER. Well, I'm off with my load of flowers. I better move fast before my little passengers start to wilt.

FLORIST. Make it snappy and try not to pass out from the aroma.

TAXI DRIVE. That Valentine's Day I was delivering flowers all over the city. Like all the other years, the heavy perfume of the flowers was a welcome change from the usual. There I was delivering expressions of love at break-neck speed to every nook and cranny in town. Until I came to my final destination.

LADY DEATH. The driver turned the last corner of his life. There he was, climbing an enormous winding staircase. One, two, three, four floors. Our poor taxi driver was out of breath. Five, six, seven floors. He was gasping for air. One last effort and another flight of stairs. Eight floors and he arrived at his last stop.

TAXI DRIVE. Jesus, that was like climbing Mount Everest.

LADY DEATH. The Valentine's Day carnations were still smiling splendidly, seemingly full of life.

TAXI DRIVER. Excuse me, are you Miss Rosalinda?

ROSALINDA. *(Entering.)* That's me. Can't you tell I'm big-hearted Rosalinda? Can't you tell I'm nice and sweet?

TAXI DRIVER. Of course, Miss. I can see how sweet you are by your eyes and mouth and smile.

ROSALINDA. And why do you suppose I'm so sweet?

TAXI DRIVER. Because this bouquet of carnations is addressed to you.

ROSALINDA. And who could have sent it? I'm a respectable girl.

TAXI DRIVER. Well it says here on the card: "For sweet Rosalinda on Valentine's Day." It is signed, "An Anonymous Admirer."

ROSALINDA. I wonder if it's Jorge, Edmundo, Nicolás, Arturo, José, Luis, Ismael, Roberto, Ignacio or Francisco.

TAXI DRIVER. *(Counting the carnations.)* Jorge, Edmundo, Nicolás, Arturo, José, Luis, Ismael, Roberto, Ignacio or Francisco...What a coincidence. Nine carnations and nine lovers. How extraordinary!

ROSALINDA. It can't be. There must be some mistake.

TAXI DRIVER. No, Miss. The address and the name are correct. So take your flowers and sign this receipt.

ROSALINDA. But I have TEN lovers.

TAXI DRIVER. Ten. Chihuahua! What a woman! She's too much!

ROSALINDA. That's me.

ANASTASIO. *(Entering.)* My name is Anastasio Carnation. Number ten on Rosalinda's list. I'm the one who snaps his fingers around here. I'm the owner of this little institution. This young lady is private property. So run along with your little flowers.

ROSALINDA. But darling, this is Valentine's Day. Have a heart! You know mine is so big it could break into ten pieces!

ANASTASIO. *(To the taxi driver.)* You better get out of here...

TAXI DRIVER. Well, I'm not playing the corpse in this little funeral. I just deliver flowers. Keep me out of this.

ROSALINDA. Those carnations were sent to me.

ANASTASIO. Give me those carnations. And as for you, you're going to get it!

TAXI DRIVER. For what?

ANASTASIO. For being a lovey-dovey messenger. *(Anastasio starts beating the taxi driver with the bouquet.)*

ROSALINDA. *(Shouting out the name of a lover with each stroke.)* Jorge, Edmundo, Nicolas, Arturo, José, Luis, Ismael, Ignacio, Roberto, Francisco. *(The taxi driver loses his balance and falls down the stairs.)*

LA CATRINA. Like a windmill, the taxi driver spins down the stairs. He falls down the infinite labyrinth of death. As he falls, the bright-colored lights of his past flash by like instant photographs.

TAXI DRIVER. I'm falling into the labyrinth of the beyond. I'm knocked against the cement and granite stairs. I forget the pain as I recall the good times in my life. Everything ends except the labyrinth and its infinite spiral.

LA CATRINA. The infinite spiral. That's where we all go down. And with the magical number of seven deaths, the Fickle Finger of Lady Death ceases to resound in the theater. And the song, that cry we'll all sing some day, that laughing of ours in the face of death, is heard no more. Silence! It's the final chorus. The sweet singing of our end, or of our beginning...

TAXI DRIVER. *(Singing.)* Adiós, muchachos, compañeros de mi vida. Barra querida de aquellos tiempos...*(The other players who have died on stage enter and approach him. They all sing.)*

ALL. Me toca a mí emprender la retirada.
Debo alejarme de mi buena muchachada.
Adiós, muchachos, ya me voy y me resigno.
Contra el destino nadie la talla.
Se terminaron para mí todas las farras.
Mi cuerpo enfermo no resiste más...
(Goodbye buddies, pals, chums who I once knew.
My time has come, my days are through.
Understand that from now on I must retire.
And spend my nights in a rocker by the fire.
Adieu, old buddies, I am leaving, I resign.
No more parties, women or wine.
I hear cruel destiny a knocking at my door.
My weary body can resist no more...)

THE END

MURDER WITH MALICE

(The Case of Santos Rodríguez)

by

VICTOR HUGO RASCON BANDA

TRANSLATED FROM THE SPANISH

by

CARLOS MORTON

Based on a true story which took place on July 24, 1973 in Dallas, Texas. This play originally premiered with the title, THE CASE OF SANTOS, on the twentieth anniversary of the tragedy of Santos Rodríguez. MURDER WITH MALICE, the second version, premiered in Mexico City at the Julio Castillo Theater under the direction of Enrique Piñeda on May 19, 1994.

CHARACTERS

RUBEN SANDOVAL, *27 years old, civil rights attorney*

BESSIE RODRIGUEZ, *40 years old, dark skinned, Mexican features*

DAVID RODRIGUEZ, *14 years old, Chicano*

SANTOS RODRIGUEZ, *12 years old, Chicano*

EL ABUELO, *80 years old, Chicano*

MULDER, *District Attorney, Anglo*

BURLESON, *Defense Attorney for Darrell Cain, Anglo*

DARRELL CAIN, *30 years old, Dallas policeman*

JUDGE

POLICEMAN

THE SCENE

Texas, 1970s

BREAKDOWN OF SCENES

I. A TRUE STORY

RUBEN. *(Entering and speaking directly to the audience.)* When you're born into a large Mexican family of 7 or 9 members, the price you pay for living in the United States is that one or two kids usually come out delinquents, with the legal system, with the police. It's the price we, the Hispanic family, has to pay to exist.

The case of Santos Rodríguez...is a true story. I was there, I know what happened. I'm Ruben Sandoval. I live in San Antonio, Texas. I became a civil rights attorney in a community where you ain't worth nothing. What happened to that boy Santos really changed me. Those kinds of people with no resources have the need to be somebody, to be important. The need to be a heavy *bato*, a real *chingón*. That's how they grow up in the gangs, *las gangas*, those who run around hiding from the police. Like Santos Rodríguez and his brother David...or like me many years ago in the *barrio* Second Ward in El Paso, Texas...that's why I became a Civil Rights attorney, to do something for the people who the system fucks, because they feel worthless, with no money, no power.

II. HOW IT ALL STARTED

(Broken windows. An alarm goes off. Police siren. Voices talking over the radio.)

ROY ARNOLD (VOICE). I'm near the Fina gas station. In Cedar Springs.

VOICE. O.K.

ROY ARNOLD. It's closed.

VOICE. Check.

ROY ARNOLD. Someone just broke in.

VOICE. See anything?

ROY ARNOLD. There's someone in the back. Three kids. They look like Chicanos.

VOICE. Be careful.

ROY ARNOLD. They saw me. They took off running down Bookhurst.

VOICE. Check.

ROY ARNOLD. I'm going after them.

VOICE. Be careful.

(A police siren is heard even louder. Six shots are fired and the sound of tires pealing on the pavement.)

ROY ARNOLD. I lost them. But I know them. I know where they live.

VOICE. Make a report.

ROY ARNOLD. I'm going to their house on Pearl Street, almost on the corner with Wolf.

VOICE. What area?

ROY ARNOLD. Little Mexico.

VOICE. O.K. Good luck and be careful.

(The sounds of the radio and the sound of the siren get lower and then fade out.)

III. I DON'T KNOW WHAT HAPPENED

CAIN. I honestly don't know what happened. I'm just like everyone else. I never miss work. I go to the gym every day. Saturdays I like to cut the grass and watch football with my son. I don't do drugs or drink. Well, once in a while a whiskey or two. If it's beer I drink Lone Star. I go to the movies, but just the Westerns. I save my money. I never get mad. Well, yes. I get mad when things don't go the way they're supposed to. I feel bad. I can't sleep. I'll never forget that night. It was two thirty in the morning and everything seemed normal. I was giving a motorist a ticket for speeding when I heard Roy Arnold over the radio say he was chasing two thieves. That's when my life changed. After that, I couldn't believe they arrested me and took me to the Dallas Police Station. Then they read me my rights and took away my badge and I.D. That's when it really hit me!

IV. A FOURTEEN-YEAR-OLD WITNESS

MULDER. Will you tell us your name?

DAVID. David Rodríguez.

MULDER. All right, David, you are going to have to speak up just a little bit so that the last lady and gentleman on the jury can hear everything that you have to say. How old are you?

DAVID. Fourteen.

MULDER. Are you in school there in Dallas?

DAVID. I'm in junior high school.

MULDER. What grade are you in, David?

DAVID. Eighth.

MULDER. How many children are there in your family?

DAVID. Five.

MULDER. Will you tell the jurors the names of your brothers and your sisters?

DAVID. Santos, Ruben, Robert, Juanita and me.

MULDER. Are you the oldest of the children?

DAVID. Yes, sir.

MULDER. How old was Santos during his lifetime?

DAVID. Twelve.

MULDER. How old are the others?

DAVID. Juanita nine, Ruben five, and Robert four.

MULDER. Your brothers, Ruben and Robert, did they live with you at that time?

DAVID. No, sir.

MULDER. Where did they live?

DAVID. I think they lived in an orphanage.

MULDER. Okay, will you tell us where you and Santos lived last summer?

DAVID. In our house in Dallas with our grandfather.

MULDER. Your grandfather is Carlos Minez?

DAVID. Yes, sir.

MULDER. And he is an eighty-year-old man, is he not?

DAVID. Yes, sir.

MULDER. What sort of work did your grandfather do?

DAVID. He used to paint houses and cut other people's grass.

MULDER. Did he work every day?

DAVID. Except Saturdays and Sundays.

MULDER. Now, David, we want to go back in time to last summer, to the day before Santos was killed.

BURLESON. Objection! The state is attempting to qualify the unfortunate death of Santos Rodríguez as a murder.

MULDER. Very well...let's go back to the time Santos Rodríguez suffered his "unfortunate death." Do you remember what time Mr. Carlos Minez came back from work?

DAVID. I don't remember...it was almost night.

MULDER. What happened then?

DAVID. He fixed supper, we ate, and then Santos and I went out to play.

MULDER. Where did you go?

DAVID. Pikes Park.

MULDER. How far is Pikes Park from your house?

DAVID. About three blocks.

MULDER. David, you are going to have to speak up a little bit louder, okay?

DAVID. Yes, sir.

MULDER. Now, what did you and Santos do at Pikes Park?

DAVID. We went to play pool in a hall inside the park.

MULDER. The area in which you lived is primarily a Mexican American area, is it not?

DAVID. Yes, sir.

MULDER. What time did you leave Pikes Park that evening?

DAVID. Around eight o'clock.

MULDER. And where did you go?

DAVID. Little Mexico Village projects.

MULDER. David, you are going to have to keep your voice up so everybody can hear what you say, even if it means yelling. Why don't you talk like you want these people back here to hear what you are saying? Okay? How far is Little Mexico from your house?

DAVID. One block.

MULDER. And what did you do when you got to Little Mexico?

DAVID. We played football.

MULDER. Is it lighted so that you can see at night?

DAVID. Yes, sir.

MULDER. What color shirt did Santos have on?

DAVID. Orange and gold.

MULDER. Did it have sleeves?

DAVID. Short sleeves.

MULDER. The boys that you were playing with were how old, approximately?

DAVID. Fifteen.

MULDER. Fifteen? And about what time did you leave Little Mexico and where did you go when you left?

DAVID. I left around 10:00 and went home.

MULDER. And where did your brother, Santos, go?

DAVID. Went to walk my cousin Herman to his house.

MULDER. How old is your cousin Herman?

DAVID. Twelve years old.

MULDER. When you got home was your grandfather there?

DAVID. Yes, sir, he was asleep.

MULDER. What did you do?

DAVID. I took off my shirt and went to bed.

MULDER. Only the shirt?

DAVID. Also my shoes.

MULDER. Did all of you sleep in the same room?

DAVID. No. Santos and I slept in the back bedroom.

MULDER. And Mr. Carlos Minez?

DAVID. On the living room sofa.

MULDER. What time did Santos come home?

DAVID. A little while after I did.

MULDER. Was he nervous or afraid?

DAVID. No.

MULDER. He came on to bed?

DAVID. Yes, sir.

MULDER. Is your house air conditioned?

DAVID. No.

MULDER. Is it hot in the summer?

DAVID. Yes, sir.

MULDER. Now, did you fall asleep, David?

DAVID. Completely.

MULDER. You recall someone with a flashlight shaking you?

DAVID. Yes.

MULDER. Did that wake you up?

DAVID. Yes.

MULDER. What did you see when you woke up?

DAVID. Two people.

MULDER. What did they do when they woke you up?

DAVID. Got me out of bed and handcuffed me.

MULDER. Did they handcuff your hands in front of you?

DAVID. No, behind my back.

MULDER. Show the jury how they handcuffed you! *(He does it.)* I want the ladies and gentlemen of the jury to note that according to normal procedures, only subjects considered highly dangerous are handcuffed behind their backs. Now, the person who handcuffed you, he had a policeman's uniform on?

DAVID. Yes, sir.

MULDER. Was your grandfather present when this occurred?

DAVID. Yes, sir.

MULDER. Did he say anything to the police?

DAVID. No.

MULDER. And the police? Did they say anything to you as to why they had come into your house so early in the morning, gotten you out of bed and handcuffed you?

DAVID. They said we were under arrest for robbery.

MULDER. And what did you say?

DAVID. We didn't say anything.

MULDER. David, is the officer who handcuffed you in the courtroom?

DAVID. Yes, sir.

MULDER. Will you please point him out to us? *(David points at Cain.)* You are pointing to *(As Mulder approaches Cain.)* this man?

DAVID. Yes, that's him.

MULDER. Very good! Please note that the witness David Rodríguez has pointed to the defendant in this case, Officer Darrell Cain.

V. HOW THE MOTHER FOUND OUT

RUBEN. *(Enters and approaches Bessie, who is behind bars.)* Are you Bessie?

BESSIE. Yes, sir.

RUBEN. I'm Ruben Sandoval, civil rights attorney.

BESSIE. Civil rights you say?

RUBEN. Yes, we defend people who claim they were abused by the police.

BESSIE. And so?

RUBEN. I'm here to see you.

BESSIE. Are you going to get me out of here?

RUBEN. Well, no...what I mean is...it'll be a temporary pass. I'll have to get special permission.

BESSIE. I don't understand.

RUBEN. You mean nobody told you...

BESSIE. What?

RUBEN. There was a burglary at a Fina gas station.

BESSIE. I heard it on the radio. But they caught the burglars, didn't they? A couple of Mexican gangbangers.

RUBEN. That's right.

BESSIE. Bunch of dumb *batos*. What do I care?

RUBEN. Bessie, those *batos* were Santos and David, your sons.

BESSIE. It's not true, it can't be true.

RUBEN. I'm sorry, but that's the way it is.

BESSIE. Oh, my God!

RUBEN. David is O.K., but Santos...

BESSIE. What happened to Santos?

RUBEN. He's dead...

BESSIE. Santos, Santos, Santos.

RUBEN. A policeman killed him. *(Beat.)*

BESSIE. Why a policeman?

RUBEN. The policeman will pay for what he did. I'll represent your family and we'll sue him, you're not alone.

VI. BESSIE'S PRAYER

Do you hear me, Santos?
Do my words reach you?
Santos, this night
I'm going to scale the walls that ring my cell.
Here, I am alone,
among women who look at me with pity
as I wait behind bars for the right moment
to fly towards you.
I see you, Santos,
I see you from here,
like watching a child going off in the morning
on the road to school.
I don't say anything.
What can I say to you,
after being lost in corridors and cells
between shadows and bars?
What can I say to you?
They took away my voice in Huntsville.
Even though you don't believe me,
I've been thinking of you.
And tonight, the doors are open,
outside there is a car,
that will take my soul to your body,
my body to your soul,
my eyes to your face, your face to my eyes.
They have clipped your wings,

they have closed your eyes,
they have imprisoned you in a box
and I can't take you out.
What will you do when you see me?
What will I do when I see you?
Perhaps you will blame me,
because I wasn't close enough
to stop that plated bullet?
Don't speak now.
Listen to me.
Just feel, just feel me,
as though you were still alive,
as though your child's soul still lived in
our house on Pearl Street, in Little Mexico.
Can you hear me, Santos...Santos...Santos?

VII. BESSIE BLAMES THE ABUELO

(The Abuelo waits anxiously for Bessie. Bessie enters and stops. They look at each other for an instant. The Abuelo tries to embrace her. Bessie shrugs him off and walks away.)

ABUELO. Daughter...

BESSIE. I don't want to see you.

ABUELO. Now just a minute, Bessie...

BESSIE. Where are my children?

ABUELO. Calm down, Bessie, listen to me!

BESSIE. I don't want to calm down.

ABUELO. You have to understand...

BESSIE. You said you would take care of them, Papa. What do you have to say about that?

ABUELO. What do I have to say?

BESSIE. Don't worry, you said, I'll take care of them. And where are they now? One in jail. The other in the funeral home.

ABUELO. There's nothing you can do, Bessie, nothing.

BESSIE. Don't tell me that.

ABUELO. I'm suffering also.

BESSIE. I want my kids back, Papa.

ABUELO. Hear me out before you blame me. Who are you to judge? What have you done with your life? What kind of example have you been to your children?

BESSIE. Why did you let them take my children away?

ABUELO. What do you want me to say? I was awake. Old people can't sleep. I looked out the window and saw a squad car stop in front of the house. Who are they looking for? What did the Martinez's do now? When the police come to the barrio and knock on the door, it is because somebody did something wrong. The police are the ones who keep order, the law. They knocked on the door. I opened it. "Where are the boys?" one of them asked. They didn't ask my permission to enter. They just went into the room where they were sleeping. What have my grandchildren done now, I thought. They took them away. What could I do? They're the police.

BESSIE. Why did you let them run around and get into trouble?

ABUELO. How could I take care of them? And work and cook!

BESSIE. Didn't you know they were getting into trouble?

ABUELO. No, but on the eve of the crime, I had a premonition.

VIII. ON THE EVE

(The Abuelo appears with a frying pan in his hand. It is apparent that he has been cooking. He puts some salt in the pan and stirs the mixture. Enter David and Santos, who cross in front of the Abuelo. He stops them.)

ABUELO. What, is there no school today?

SANTOS. There's always school.

ABUELO. I mean classes. Aren't there any classes?

DAVID. *(To Santos, joking.)* Do we have classes today?

SANTOS. *(Feigning ignorance.)* Who knows.

ABUELO. What do you mean "who knows?" Why aren't you in school?

DAVID. Because we're here.

SANTOS. We are on our way to Pike's Park.

ABUELO. What Pike's Park! Sit down.

DAVID. We have to go. They're waiting for us.

ABUELO. I said sit down! *(David and Santos obey, but are obviously displeased.)* You are both underage. And I have the final say in this house. I work myself to death. I give you food and a roof over your head. And all I ask is that you go to school. Is that asking too much? Do you want to be poor, dumb beasts of burden all your life? Worthless good-for-nothings?

SANTOS. We don't like school.

ABUELO. You do what's best, not what's easy.

DAVID. They treat us bad.

ABUELO. Who?

SANTOS. The teachers.

ABUELO. What do they say?

SANTOS. They always criticize us. They punish us for nothing. For speaking Spanish.

ABUELO. You have to obey them. Speak English there and Spanish here at home.

SANTOS. They say we don't speak English or Spanish.

DAVID. They say we speak *Tex Mex*.

SANTOS. Like *Pochos*.

DAVID. You mean *Spanglish*.

ABUELO. So what? You go there to learn, not to be babied.

SANTOS. You don't understand, we have real problems.

ABUELO. What kind of problems?

DAVID. They don't like us because we're Chicanos.

ABUELO. I like you. Your mother loves you.

SANTOS. Don't play dumb, Abuelo. You know what we mean.

DAVID. You know what? Sometimes I wish I was an American.

ABUELO. You are an American. You were born here.

DAVID. I'm a Chicano, Abuelo. My name is Rodríguez, not Williams or Brown, like the others.

SANTOS. The damn teacher said yesterday that the Mexicans are invading Texas. That they're going to put up a big iron fence all along the border. That they come to take jobs away from real Americans.

ABUELO. Do you believe that?

DAVID. I do.

SANTOS. I don't.

ABUELO. The gringos have only been here a short time. We've been living here longer than they have. See the difference?

SANTOS. How do you know all that?

ABUELO. Last night I heard it on the radio. A man named Tino Villanueva said it.

SANTOS. I don't believe you.

ABUELO. Haven't you noticed the names of the streets and the cities? El Paso, Los Angeles, San Antonio? Don't let them feed you lies. Mexicans gave to the land. We have the right to be here. You should be proud to be a Rodríguez. Now, are you going to go to school tomorrow? *(David and Santos look at each other without replying.)* I asked you a question. Are you going?

SANTOS. Maybe, maybe not.

DAVID. We'll think about it.

ABUELO. *(The Abuelo takes off his belt and shows it to them.)* Look here, you good-for-nothings, you better go to school. Do you hear me?

DAVID. O.K. You don't have to do that.

ABUELO. *(To Santos.)* And you?

SANTOS. Yes.

ABUELO. Yes, what?

SANTOS. Yes, sir.

DAVID. Can we go back to park now?

ABUELO. Heck no, I'm still mad at you.

SANTOS. Please, Abuelo!

ABUELO. All right, but don't be long.

SANTOS. What are you going to make for dinner?

ABUELO. For you, nothing. You don't deserve it, for being such bad boys.

SANTOS. I want a hamburger, so don't give us any darn tacos or tamales, because the teacher says that's why we are so ugly.

ABUELO. David! Santos! You better get home early. Don't get in any trouble! *(Santos and David exit. The Abuelo watches them to off with sadness.)* Those kids! *(He has a premonition.)* After they left I felt something wrong, like fear, as though...Bessie, forgive me...

IX. HOW THE JURY WAS FORMED

RUBEN. The policeman is going to be tried in Austin because if they tried him in Dallas there would be too many Chicanos on the jury.

BESSIE. I was tried by a jury of gringos. I want that man to be tried by a jury of Chicanos.

RUBEN. Dream on, Bessie, it isn't going to happen.

BESSIE. And why not? Chicanos are citizens too. They pay taxes. Why can't they serve on the jury?

RUBEN. The system works this way. Suppose they call some Chicanos to the court. You go and they ask you if you read something about this case in the newspapers. Yes. Out you go because you've already formed an opinion. Here comes another Chicano. Do you speak English? Uh, not very well. Then out you go. Do you have small children, they ask? Yes, two. Out you go. And here comes a real heavy *bato*, very sure of himself. Are you registered to vote? Well, no. Then, if you're not registered to vote, you can't be on the jury. You don't exist. You're not worth a damn. That's the way it is, Bessie, Chicanos don't register to vote. That's why we don't exist.

BESSIE. We're screwed.

RUBEN. We have to do something. In Austin, an all white jury will never find a white man guilty.

X. I JUST CAN'T GET IT OUT OF MY MIND

CAIN. They can't send me to prison, can they? What will happen to my wife? What will happen to my kids? After I get out I won't have a job, all my savings will be used up, I won't have a future. Here in Austin the press is accusing me all the time. The reporters followed my wife with their television cameras into the bathroom. If they lock me up no one will want to be a cop, no one will respect us ever again. I respect the rights of those people. Just as long as they don't leave the *barrio*. Just as long as they don't come where they're not wanted. As long as they don't steal. Or kill. What did I do wrong? I don't like their food, their music, dances, language. They're greasy, lying, dirty, stupid. What good will it do to send me to prison? Jail is a school for crime. What will I do in jail with a bunch of thieves and killers I helped capture? It's humiliating! Put yourself in my place! In one brief instant the course of your life changed forever! I wish this were but a dream that upon waking, had never happened! I am not a bad person! Don't let them find me guilty, Burleson! I am not a killer. I swear it!

XI. I DIDN'T MEAN TO DO IT

BURLESON. State your name.

CAIN. Darrell Cain.

BURLESON. How old are you?

CAIN. Thirty-four.

BURLESON. Where do you live?

CAIN. In Midlothian, Texas, outside of Dallas.

BURLESON. Do you live there with your wife?

CAIN. Yes, I do.

BURLESON. And two children?

CAIN. That's correct.

BURLESON. How old are your children?

CAIN. I have a little boy six and a little girl two.

BURLESON. All right. Were you in the U.S. Army?

CAIN. Yes.

BURLESON. Vietnam?

CAIN. Yes, sir.

BURLESON. Did you volunteer or were you drafted?

CAIN. I volunteered.

BURLESON. How long were you in the service?

CAIN. For three years.

BURLESON. Were you honorably discharged?

CAIN. Yes, I was.

BURLESON. We are not judging a criminal, but rather a citizen like us, perhaps better than us. Now, directing your attention to the month of July, what shift were you working?

CAIN. I was working from 11:00 p.m. until 7:00 o'clock in the morning.

BURLESON. Would you explain to the jury what a police officer does while covering a district?

CAIN. Well, he drives a patrol car and he has a certain area which is his assigned beat. He covers that area and answers calls when people call in for assistance.

BURLESON. In the early morning hours of July 24, 1973, did you hear a radio transmission of Roy Arnold's that he had chased some burglars who had just held up a gas station?

CAIN. Yes, sir, I did.

BURLESON. All right. What did you do then?

CAIN. I headed in the direction where Officer Arnold had last seen the suspects running.

BURLESON. Were you still monitoring your radio?

CAIN. Yes.

BURLESON. What else did you hear?

CAIN. Arnold said that he had last seen the suspects running up Bookhurst and that he was going to follow them.

BURLESON. Where did you go then?

CAIN. Pearl Street.

BURLESON. Did you have a conversation with Roy Arnold then?

CAIN. Yes, he believed the suspects lived in a house on that street.

BURLESON. He thought the suspects lived here. Did anything else happen?

CAIN. I heard a call stating that the back window of the service station had been broken into.

BURLESON. All right. What did you do in response to that?

CAIN. I got out of the car and went over to where Officer Arnold was.

BURLESON. Where was he?

CAIN. Inside the residence.

BURLESON. Did you see the grandfather in there?

CAIN. Yes, sir.

BURLESON. Where did the two of you go then?

CAIN. We went through the first room and into the second room.

BURLESON. How were they dressed?

CAIN. One of them had on a pair of underpants, socks, a white undershirt. The other one had on a pair of underpants, socks and he was bare chested.

BURLESON. What happened next?

CAIN. Officer Arnold told me that these were the boys he had been chasing. So, we got them up out of bed and advised them that we were arresting them for burglary.

BURLESON. Could you tell the ladies and gentlemen of the jury their condition as you saw them?

CAIN. Yes, sir; they had a considerable amount of sweat on them.

BURLESON. Did you have any difficulty waking them up?

CAIN. No, we didn't.

BURLESON. Which led you to believe that they were pretending to be asleep.

MULDER. Objection. The defense is putting words in the mouth of the accused.

BURLESON. After Roy Arnold said those were the boys that he saw running from the service station, what did you then do?

CAIN. We arrested them and took them outside.

BURLESON. All right. Were the boys handcuffed at any time?

CAIN. Yes, as soon as we got them up out of bed.

BURLESON. Is it normal police procedure to handcuff people under those circumstances?

CAIN. Yes, sir, it is.

BURLESON. Is that what you are taught and trained to do?

CAIN. Yes, sir.

BURLESON. After taking them out of the house, where did you put them? In the car?

CAIN. Yes, sir.

BURLESON. Whose car?

CAIN. Officer Arnold's.

BURLESON. In Arnold's car, you were seated in the left rear, Santos was in the right front, David was in the right rear and Roy Arnold was driving, right?

CAIN. That's correct.

BURLESON. Did you order Roy Arnold to go anywhere?

CAIN. He was driving; he went where he wanted to.

BURLESON. Roy Arnold stopped at the parking lot on the back of the Fina station. Is that correct?

CAIN. Yes, sir.

BURLESON. Tell us what happened after you got there.

CAIN. We heard information that there was probably three suspects involved in this burglary.

BURLESON. What happened next?

CAIN. Officer Arnold turned to Santos and asked him if he had a brother.

BURLESON. What was the response?

CAIN. Santos told him that he did have a brother.

BURLESON. What was said then?

CAIN. Officer Arnold asked him if he knew where his brother was.

BURLESON. What was said in response to that?

CAIN. He said he didn't know.

BURLESON. What was said after that?

CAIN. If I recall correctly, I said, "I will make him tell the truth."

BURLESON. And when you said that, what did you do?

CAIN. I took my pistol out of my holster.

BURLESON. Where was your pistol? On your right side?

CAIN. Yes, sir.

BURLESON. And when you took your pistol out of the holster, what did you do then?

CAIN. I stuck it down between my legs and emptied it.

BURLESON. Did it make any type of noise?

CAIN. Yes, sir, I believe it probably did.

BURLESON. The noise of the bullets hitting together?

CAIN. Yes.

BURLESON. What did you do next?

CAIN. I glanced at the cylinder.

BURLESON. Where were you holding the gun at the time that you glanced at the cylinder?

CAIN. Between my legs.

BURLESON. What did you do with the bullets that came out of the gun?

CAIN. Placed them between my legs.

BURLESON. When you looked at the cylinder, did you see anything?

CAIN. No, sir.

BURLESON. Is your gun nickel plated?

CAIN. Yes, sir, it is.

BURLESON. The bullets in your gun, were they silver?

CAIN. Yes, sir.

BURLESON. Obviously, it was easy to confuse them. After you looked in the cylinder, what did you do next?

CAIN. I closed the cylinder.

BURLESON. Then what did you do?

CAIN. I pointed it at the boy.

XII. IT WAS AN ACCIDENT

BURLESON. And as you pointed it at Santos, what did you do then?

CAIN. I told him to tell the truth.

BURLESON. What next?

CAIN. I pulled the trigger.

BURLESON. What happened?

CAIN. Nothing, it just clicked.

BURLESON. At the time that you did that, was it your belief that the pistol was totally empty?

CAIN. Yes, sir.

BURLESON. What happened after you pulled the trigger the first time?

CAIN. I told him, "Tell the truth, there is another bullet in the gun."

BURLESON. What was said or done next?

CAIN. I pulled the trigger.

BURLESON. What happened the second time?

CAIN. The gun went off.

BURLESON. What happened after the gun went off?

CAIN. I jumped from the car.

BURLESON. What did you do with the bullets that were in your lap?

CAIN. Repeat the question, please.

BURLESON. What happened to the bullets that were in your lap?

CAIN. I picked them up.

BURLESON. What did you do then?

CAIN. Jumped from the car.

BURLESON. Then what did you do with the bullets?

MULDER. Objection. The defense is leading the witness.

BURLESON. But his answer is important.

CAIN. I put them in the cylinder again.

BURLESON. What was your state of mind at that time? What were you doing?

CAIN. I was screaming, crying.

BURLESON. Do you remember anything that you said immediately after the shooting?

CAIN. Really, about all I can remember is what I have read in the papers.

BURLESON. Roy Arnold testified that he heard you say, "Roy, I didn't mean to do it." Do you remember saying anything like that?

CAIN. Yes, you're right, that's what I said.

BURLESON. When you held the gun up to the head of Santos Rodríguez, did you know there was a bullet in there?

CAIN. No, I didn't know there was a bullet in there.

BURLESON. And would you tell the ladies and gentlemen of the jury whether or not it was an accident that the bullet got stuck in the chamber.

CAIN. It was accidental.

XIII. SANTOS VISITS THE ABUELO AND DAVID

(The Abuelo is asleep in a rocker. Something wakes him up. Someone calls to him from the darkness.)

VOICE (OFF). Pssst...psttt.

ABUELO. *(Looking with fear all around him.)* Who's there?

VOICE. Abuelo.

ABUELO. Who is it?

VOICE. It's me...Santos, Santos.

ABUELO. Oh, dear God! For the pain that you suffered in the Via Crucis, have pity on the lost souls and in particular the soul of this poor innocent child who is suffering so much. Have pity on him!

SANTOS. Pssst. Psst. David.

DAVID. What do you want?

SANTOS. I came to see you.

DAVID. Go away!

SANTOS. You don't want to see me?

DAVID. No.

SANTOS. I want to talk to you.

ABUELO. What are you doing here? You should be resting.

SANTOS. I'm not tired.

ABUELO. What do you want?

SANTOS. To be with you.

ABUELO. You shouldn't be here. Go back from where you came.

SANTOS. Help me.

ABUELO. How? What's wrong with you?

SANTOS. I'm lost.

ABUELO. That's how it is at first...

DAVID. I'm afraid of you.

SANTOS. I'm your brother, David.

DAVID. You were my brother...

SANTOS. I am your brother.

DAVID. And the blood?

SANTOS. They washed my head.

DAVID. And the handcuffs?

SANTOS. They took them off.

DAVID. That's not your clothes.

SANTOS. They put new clothes on me.

DAVID. Who?

SANTOS. I don't know. I came back for you.

DAVID. Why?

SANTOS. I want to play in Pike's Park.

DAVID. I can't.

SANTOS. I don't know what to do...

ABUELO. That's what happens to people who die violently. Their soul cannot move on. Although, eventually the soul finds its way.

SANTOS. Help me, Abuelo, help me.

ABUELO. I'll help you. It's just that we didn't pray for your soul. Back in Mexico people pray nine days so the soul can rest in peace. Here we've forgotten how to do it. But you'll have your prayers, you'll see. And we'll go visit you on the Day of the Dead. We'll put up an altar of flowers with candles and your favorite foods. I promise.

DAVID. What did it feel like getting shot?

SANTOS. When?

DAVID. In the patrol car. Did it hurt?

SANTOS. It was like a brilliant flash, like lightening. Then...*(He says nothing.)*

DAVID. What happened next?

SANTOS. At first I was sad. Then I felt like going back. Now you tell me what happened.

ABUELO. You left us.

SANTOS. I didn't want to go.

ABUELO. You were the first one to leave us.

SANTOS. Why me, Abuelo?

ABUELO. It was God's will.

SANTOS. Why did you let them take me that night?

ABUELO. I didn't know what they were going to do.

SANTOS. Why didn't you stop them?

ABUELO. What can an old man of eighty years, who doesn't even know English, do? I thought you had done something bad. It was the police.

SANTOS. And God? Where was God? Why didn't He help me?

ABUELO. I don't know where God was.

SANTOS. *(To David.)* Do you remember my new tennis shoes that were a couple of sizes too big for me?

DAVID. Yes.

SANTOS. And that I hid them from you?

DAVID. Yes.

SANTOS. And that I never let you borrow them?

DAVID. Yes.

SANTOS. They're yours now! You'll find them in the Abuelo's suitcase. *(To the Abuelo.)* Do you love me?

ABUELO. A lot. And I miss you.

SANTOS. Me, too. Take care of David.

ABUELO. Don't worry.

SANTOS. And my Mother, too.

ABUELO. I'll watch over her.

SANTOS. I feel all alone.

ABUELO. We will be together soon. I'll come after you.

SANTOS. Really?

ABUELO. But you better go now.

SANTOS. Can I come back again?

ABUELO. No, you have to rest. I'll go and visit you every day.

SANTOS. Will you, Abuelo, will you?

ABUELO. Oh, all powerful God, for the love that you feel for mankind, and for the agony you suffered, have pity on the poor souls who wander lost in Purgatory.

DAVID. I've got to get out of here. I'm going to kill him. I'm going to kill that cop. I hate him. I hate all the police. When I get out of here I'm going to kill all of them. I hate them. Santos...Santos...Santos...

XIV. I KNOW WHO THEY ARE

RUBEN. Do you see, Don Carlos, those sons of bitches don't know the law. They think they know everything. When someone commits a crime they go visit all the known suspects. All the ones who would be capable of doing it. That's what happened to your grandsons. That's what Roy Arnold thought early one July morning when he saw three boys running away. He shot at them. They got away. Then he thought: I know them. I know David and Santos. Those punks love to get into trouble. Little rats. I know where they live. And so Arnold and Cain went looking for them. And you opened the door? Is that what happened?

ABUELO. What? Do you think I invited them into my house? They just walked right in! Bessie said the same thing. Poor Bessie. My daughter isn't a bad person. She's just had a lot of bad luck. She's gone from one failure to another.

XV. THE PAST, BESSIE'S FAILURES

BESSIE. I killed him; so what? What's the deal? I'm here, paying for it.

RUBEN. You shouldn't be behind bars.

BESSIE. But I killed him.

RUBEN. You must have had your reasons.

BESSIE. Plenty of reasons. It was him or me. His death was my life.

RUBEN. Was he your husband?

BESSIE. No. We had lived together for a year. His name was Leonard Brown. He was a son of a bitch.

RUBEN. Why did you live with him?

BESSIE. At first, because I liked him. I needed a father for my five sons. In the past...well, I had lots of failures. My first failure was David and Santos' father. I was very young and very much in love. His name was David. A real *macho*, the *cabrón*. He was from Jalisco. He left me and went back to Mexico. One day he left to buy cigarettes and never came back. I don't even want to think about it. He left me. That's the way it is. I needed a man in the house, someone the boys could respect. You understand?

RUBEN. Then you put up with Leonard Brown for convenience's sake?

BESSIE. I guess so, if you want to know the truth. I put up with that fucker for a long time. He would give me money and other things. Money and kicks, money and threats, money and slaps across the face. He was a mean old fucker, a mafioso.

RUBEN. Did you plan his death?

BESSIE. Of course not. We had an argument one day, like always. The bastard tried to cut me with a knife. I grabbed his pistol from the bureau. I emptied the cartridge. The boys were crying. The man fell at my feet and I kept loading the pistol, just in case he got up. I was really afraid of him. The police came. They handcuffed me. They arrested me, booked me, tried me, and sentenced me. Five years. Five years in hell!

RUBEN. And your children?

BESSIE. They were adopted, like dogs without an owner, by families they didn't know. The three little ones, I mean. The older boys, Santos and David, they went to live with their grandfather, my father. Nobody wanted them. Imagine! An eighty-year-old man. What could the poor man do?

RUBEN. And no one said you acted in self defense?

BESSIE. What do you mean? Self defense?

RUBEN. That you were just defending yourself.

BESSIE. No. Nobody told me nothing. How could I pay for a lawyer? The State named one for me. He did what he could.

RUBEN. No. If they had put up a good defense you wouldn't have set foot in jail.

BESSIE. Come on, are you serious? *(Long pause.)* I believe in fate. Suddenly, fate can change our lives. And life becomes a veil of tears where once there was joy. That's how it is for many of us in the *barrio*.

XVI. I'LL MAKE YOU TELL THE TRUTH

MULDER. Cain, I want to know just what made you think you had the right to point a gun at that boy's head.

CAIN. I don't know, it was like an impulse.

MULDER. Now, you talked about normal police procedure and what you have been taught. Is that your normal police procedure?

CAIN. No.

MULDER. Were you trained to interrogate a twelve-year-old child at the end of a .357 magnum?

CAIN. No, I wasn't trained to do that.

MULDER. Then why did you point that gun at a boy's head?

CAIN. I don't know.

MULDER. Surely before using the revolver, you thought it over carefully, didn't you?

CAIN. Yes, sir.

MULDER. It's your testimony to the jury that you reached in your holster and removed your gun.

CAIN. Yes, sir.

MULDER. After stating, "I will make him tell the truth." Why did you tell Santos that?

CAIN. I don't know.

MULDER. The boy had repeatedly denied he was involved in that burglary, hadn't he?

CAIN. Yes, he had.

MULDER. Why did you set yourself up as the judge of who was telling the truth and who wasn't?

CAIN. I don't know.

MULDER. How long have you had this gun?

CAIN. Just a little over a year.

MULDER. You carried it with you all of the time, didn't you?

CAIN. Yes, I did.

MULDER. All right, and this isn't a standard gun, is it?

CAIN. No, sir.

MULDER. Got a white outlined rear sight, doesn't it?

CAIN. That's correct.

MULDER. It allows you to aim better at long range.

CAIN. Yes.

MULDER. One of the advantages of a gun like this is that you can shoot with it at night, can't you?

CAIN. Yes.

MULDER. Because you can see the white outline as you throw down on someone?

CAIN. Yes, that's correct.

MULDER. Your gun was fully loaded when you removed it from your holster that night, wasn't it?

CAIN. Yes, sir.

MULDER. In case you wanted to interrogate somebody or get the truth out of them?

CAIN. No, that's not why I kept it loaded.

MULDER. Just kept it loaded in case you wanted to shoot it?

CAIN. Yes, sir.

MULDER. You are taught at the Academy not to take your gun out of the holster unless you are going to use it, aren't you?

CAIN. Yes.

MULDER. They also teach you at the Academy that you are to protect and respect the rights of those in custody, because they are under your protection, aren't they?

CAIN. That's correct.

MULDER. You were wearing a badge and uniform that night, weren't you?

CAIN. Yes, sir.

MULDER. And you were supposed to protect anyone in your custody, weren't you?

CAIN. Yes.

MULDER. You weren't supposed to threaten them, were you?

CAIN. No, sir.

MULDER. A boy with his hands handcuffed behind him, you are not telling this jury he was trying to get away, are you?

CAIN. No, he wasn't trying to get away.

MULDER. He answered your questions, didn't he?

CAIN. Yes.

MULDER. Didn't refuse to answer any questions?

CAIN. No.

MULDER. Did you realize that the reason he couldn't tell Arnold where his other older brother was is that the boy had been placed in a foster home when Santos was five years old? Yet you thought he was lying to you, so you set yourself up as judge.

CAIN. Yes.

MULDER. You know that this gun is a six shot revolver, don't you? *(Cain looks at him strangely.)*

CAIN. I sure do.

MULDER. Will you show us how you opened the gun up? *(Cain demonstrates how he opened the gun, emphasizing his words with the action.)* This time you dumped the bullets into your hand. But that night it's your contention that one got jammed?

CAIN. Apparently so.

MULDER. Never happened before, had it?

CAIN. It never happened to me.

MULDER. During an interrogation?

CAIN. No, sir.

MULDER. You were shooting Smith and Wesson ammunition that night, weren't you?

CAIN. Yes, sir.

MULDER. Is there anything unusual about the nose of that bullet?

CAIN. It has a hollow point.

MULDER. What is a hollow point?

CAIN. It's an indentation within the lead.

MULDER. Why would you use hollow points?

CAIN. It has a little more shooting power.

MULDER. It's something that when it hits, it explodes and breaks apart?

CAIN. Yes.

MULDER. If it's at short range?

CAIN. Well, as far as I know it doesn't have to be at short range.

MULDER. Well, and you're such a great shot, aren't you?

BURLESON. Objection. The State is using sarcasm regarding this tragic and lamentable accident.

MULDER. Well, you had a gun with a white outline rear sight and a red ram front sight, a souped-up pistol.

CAIN. I have seen several police officers with the same kind of gun.

MULDER. Let me take this gun and let's see if I can go through the same motions. You watch me and see if I do this the way you say you did that night. *(He demonstrates.)* All right, you pushed the ejector like that? And held the gun up and dumped it like that? To make sure the bullets came out, right?

CAIN. The ejector was held down.

MULDER. It's your story that one bullet got hung up. But nonetheless you are trained to maneuver the gun up and then down, without having to push the ejector—so the bullets will slide out by themselves.

CAIN. Yes, I was trained to push down the ejector.

MULDER. I know you were trained...But these bullets are real slippery, they fall out without pushing the ejector. *(Beat.)* You had the bullets in your hand?

CAIN. Yes, sir.

MULDER. And the revolver?

CAIN. Excuse me?

MULDER. Did you put the bullets in your lap or on the seat?

CAIN. I just dumped them on the seat.

MULDER. Now, you say you checked the cylinder, then closed the gun.

CAIN. Well, I just glanced at it.

MULDER. All right. Of course, your story is that you wanted to make sure it was empty.

CAIN. Yes, sir.

MULDER. So you certainly saw well enough to determine whether it was empty. You thought the lighting was sufficient to determine if the gun was empty?

CAIN. I thought so; yes, sir.

MULDER. Now, you want this jury to believe that you were going to unload this gun, in front of David Rodríguez, in an effort to get the truth out of Santos Rodríguez. Don't you think David could have said to his brother, in Spanish, "Don't sweat it, Santos, the gun isn't loaded."

CAIN. He didn't.

MULDER. Your intent being to frighten both of the boys in an effort to get the truth out of them. That's your story, isn't it?

CAIN. Yes, sir, that's the story. It's the truth.

MULDER. That's only your side of the story!

XVII. I ACCUSE

BESSIE. Where have you been? Why haven't you called? Why haven't you come to see me? What are you doing!

RUBEN. The case has gotten complicated. I've been in Austin, in court, helping out the prosecution.

BESSIE. That's all?

RUBEN. That's all I can do right now. When Cain's trial is over, we'll sue the Dallas police. We'll make them pay for what they did to you and your children.

BESSIE. Is that going to make Santos come back to life?

RUBEN. No, but the State of Texas should be held liable for damages.

BESSIE. Swear they're going to find Cain guilty! Are they? *(Beat.)* You don't know? How come you don't know? Who knows, then? The judge? The jury? The Governor of Texas? The president? God? Who the fuck knows?

RUBEN. Calm down, Bessie.

BESSIE. Why does everyone ask me to calm down?

RUBEN. You're not going to get anywhere acting like this.

BESSIE. And how do you want me to act? Have they killed your son? You don't know what it's like. All you know are the courts and the law. And from the looks of it, you don't know much. Why don't you just get out of here, all right? *(Ruben starts to go.)* Wait! Do you really want to help me?

RUBEN. Yes.

BESSIE. Then get me out of here.

RUBEN. There's nothing I can do about your case. No appeals, nothing. You've been sentenced.

BESSIE. What did you say?

RUBEN. That you've been tried and sentenced.

BESSIE. Say it again!

RUBEN. *(Confused. Staring at her.)* You have to serve your time.

BESSIE. Are you sure? *(Bessie laughs.)* How do you know? *(Laughing hysterically.)* You think you really know me? *(She laughs, almost crying.)* What do you know about me, what I think, what I feel? *(She regains her composure and looks at him seriously.)* Yes, you're right. I've been sentenced. Damned for all time. Fucked. Even by God.

XVIII. I DIDN'T MAKE UP ANY STORIES

MULDER. Arnold didn't know you had your gun out, did he?

CAIN. I don't know whether he did or not.

MULDER. Well, are you saying that you and Roy cooked this interrogation method up between the two of you?

CAIN. No, sir.

MULDER. It was all your idea?

CAIN. Yes, sir.

MULDER. Why did you interrogate him in that manner?

CAIN. I don't know, it just happened, all of a sudden.

MULDER. All of a sudden! All right. You pointed the gun at Santos Rodríguez' head, so he would look at you?

CAIN. Yes, sir.

MULDER. He said, "I am telling the truth," and you made the gun click.

CAIN. Yes.

MULDER. You made that gun click and then you told him, "Tell the truth, there is a bullet in here?"

CAIN. Yes, that's correct.

MULDER. Why did you tell him that if you were sure the cylinder was empty?

CAIN. To scare him.

MULDER. My God, he must have been scared enough with you pointing the gun that close to his head.

CAIN. Yes, I suppose he would be.

MULDER. He was a twelve-year-old kid.

CAIN. Yes, he was.

MULDER. I want you to tell the jury what his last words were.

CAIN. "I am telling the truth."

MULDER. And then you pulled the trigger, ending his life, didn't you?

CAIN. Yes, I did.

MULDER. According to you there were bullets between your legs, but they didn't fall, even though the seat was smooth. Now, when you unloaded the gun, I assume your back was up against the seat, wasn't it?

CAIN. Yes, sir.

MULDER. When you pointed the gun at the child's head, you must have leaned forward like this. But strangely, the bullets didn't fall from the seat.

CAIN. I suppose not. I'm not sure.

MULDER. Now, when the gun went off, did you jump out of the car?

CAIN. I don't know whether I jumped or not.

MULDER. Everybody else jumped. Arnold said he almost jumped out of the car, because, Cain, no one expected that gun to go off. But your story is that you did not jump.

CAIN. I don't know whether I did or not.

MULDER. You don't know. Well, be as it may, you were able to reach right down and find those bullets.

CAIN. I guess I did.

MULDER. All right. Now, why on earth would you want to reload the gun? Were you going to use it again?

CAIN. It was just a reaction; I don't know why I did it.

MULDER. Come on, a reaction! Like holding the gun to the kid's head, that kind of reaction?

CAIN. I don't know.

MULDER. You want them to believe that you were surprised when the gun went off, yet you were able to reach down there between your legs, get the bullets, get out of the car, load your gun and then you became hysterical?

CAIN. I was hysterical during all of this.

MULDER. You were hysterical while you were loading the gun?

CAIN. Yes, sir, I was.

MULDER. Well, Roy Arnold said you didn't load that gun when you got out of the car; you kept the gun in your right hand. And at that moment you fell down.

CAIN. Yes, sir, I fell down and vomited.

MULDER. Then you were taken down to the Dallas Police Department, weren't you?

CAIN. Yes, that's correct.

MULDER. You were in the car with Roy Arnold?

CAIN. Yes.

MULDER. It takes fifteen minutes to get down there from the scene of the shooting to Central Headquarters where Homicide is located. Can you look the jury in the eye and tell them that you didn't discuss this?

CAIN. I haven't said we didn't discuss it.

MULDER. What is your story?

CAIN. What I'm saying is I don't know whether we did or not, really. We talked, I'm sure, but we were in shock, we were stunned.

MULDER. Arnold was able to drive, wasn't he? I mean, he made it down there without a collision.

CAIN. Yes, he was able to drive.

MULDER. I suggest that you talked about it on the way down.

CAIN. We talked, I'm sure we did. As to what was said, I don't know.

MULDER. Then you don't remember when you cooked up the story about unloading the gun in the back seat?

CAIN. I didn't cook up a story.

MULDER. You don't remember talking to your lawyer and telling him about unloading the gun?

CAIN. I don't remember when I first told somebody that.

MULDER. After you and your lawyer and Arnold talked about the facts, you came up with this story. You were so hysterical that you can't remember anything that happened after you loaded that gun?

CAIN. No, I cannot remember.

MULDER. But you knew all along, Cain, that the time would come when you would be called on to explain how that gun ended up loaded, didn't you?

CAIN. Repeat the question, please.

MULDER. You knew the day would come when you would be called on to explain why your gun was taken from your hand eight seconds after the shot was fired, with five live rounds of ammunition and one spent hull in it.

CAIN. I still don't understand the question.

MULDER. You knew you would have to account for the fact that the gun was fully loaded, didn't you?

CAIN. Yes.

MULDER. You want this jury to believe that in three or four seconds, in a hysterical condition, you were able to break this gun apart, put the bullets in it, and close it before Arnold took it from your hand?

CAIN. What I am saying is that Arnold did not immediately come and get my gun.

MULDER. What did he do? Leave you around with a gun in your hand to see if there was anybody else you wanted to interrogate?

CAIN. There was mass confusion out there. Nobody was really in his senses.

MULDER. Did you tell Mr. Burleson that the reason you reloaded your gun was that you are taught an empty gun is no use of whatsoever?

CAIN. I don't remember.

MULDER. You didn't kick the spent hull out of your gun, when you reloaded it?

CAIN. No.

MULDER. Cain, you are talking to twelve adult people; these are not twelve-year-olds you are talking to.

CAIN. Yes, I know.

MULDER. You are asking these adults to believe that you nonchalantly got out of the car? You must have been moving awfully fast.

CAIN. I was moving, but not fast.

MULDER. You are asking them to believe that you reloaded this gun in the car!

CAIN. No, I...

MULDER. Well, if you were so hell bent on reloading the gun, why didn't you do it there in the car?

CAIN. I wanted out of that car.

MULDER. No thought about Santos.

CAIN. Yes.

MULDER. You didn't reach over the seat, to see if there was anything you could do for him?

CAIN. I was in shock.

MULDER. In shock, hysterical, got out of the car, moving, loaded the gun in three to four seconds. You can't even load this gun in three or four seconds, can you?

CAIN. I can load it in probably four to six.

MULDER. I guess you can also do it so fast that nobody can see you. You are asking the jury to swallow this, that you got out of that car, opened this cylinder, loaded the gun, yet nobody saw you?

CAIN. Nobody saw me.

MULDER. Nobody. Arnold said it was loaded when he took it from your hand, as soon as you jumped out of the car.

CAIN. He didn't take it from my hand.

MULDER. Oh, so Officer Arnold is also mistaken about that too?

XIX. THE NEW BESSIE

BESSIE. You're wrong, Papa, I'm going to change.

ABUELO. You're never going to change, Bessie.

BESSIE. I know what I'm saying, Papa.

ABUELO. But you're in jail.

BESSIE. You act like you don't want me to get out of here.

ABUELO. Yes, I do. Get out so you can live in your house and take care of David.

BESSIE. And the other children too. How are they?

ABUELO. I don't know.

BESSIE. You mean you don't even know? Haven't you been to see them? I want to bring them home so they don't have to live with strangers.

ABUELO. Right now they're better off there. What if I die all of a sudden? I'm not going to last very long. And life outside is harder than in here.

BESSIE. Life has always been tough. I'll go to work. They'll have everything they need.

ABUELO. It's not going to be easy to get work, because of your record.

BESSIE. You mean I'm screwed, is that it?

ABUELO. Well, yes. To be honest about it.

BESSIE. Listen, Papa, a different Bessie is going to come out of here. Stronger than before.

ABUELO. Are you going to get caught drinking and driving?

BESSIE. No.

ABUELO. Are you going to be stubborn?

BESSIE. Not as much.

ABUELO. Are you going to keep insulting the police?

BESSIE. Only if they push me.

ABUELO. Are you going to be God fearing?

BESSIE. A bit more.

ABUELO. Are you going to think with your head?

BESSIE. Maybe, maybe not.

ABUELO. Are you going to get another boyfriend?

BESSIE. No, never again. Not on your life. Fucking men are all alike, it's their fault I'm here. I'm lucky I met Maria in here. She's not like them.

XX. WE WEREN'T THERE

BURLESON. Before the night of July 24th, had you ever seen Officer Cain?

DAVID. Just once.

BURLESON. When was that?

DAVID. Another time, burglary.

BURLESON. Ah, another burglary. Had he seen you on that occasion?

DAVID. Yes, sir.

BURLESON. Where did he see you?

DAVID. At my house.

BURLESON. *(Pointing to Cain.)* Now, is this the Officer Cain you are talking about?

DAVID. Yes, sir.

BURLESON. When was it?

DAVID. Around February.

BURLESON. Fine, let's go back to the month of July. You say it was Officer Cain that got you out of bed that night and handcuffed you?

DAVID. Yes, sir.

BURLESON. And Officer Arnold handcuffed Santos?

DAVID. Yes, sir.

BURLESON. While you were riding over in the squad car going from your house to the gas station, did Officer Cain say anything to either you or Santos or was Arnold doing all of the talking?

DAVID. I don't remember.

BURLESON. You don't remember Arnold saying that he had seen you and Santos run from behind the service station?

DAVID. I remember he told me that.

BURLESON. Have you ever told anyone that you saw Officer Arnold there at the service station and that he chased you from the service station?

DAVID. No, sir.

BURLESON. You have never told that to anyone?

DAVID. No, sir.

BURLESON. Did you ever tell a reporter that when Officer Arnold was chasing you from the service station that he used vulgar language or curse words with you?

DAVID. I heard something like that.

BURLESON. You heard something like that?

DAVID. Yes, sir.

BURLESON. My question, David, is: Did you tell a reporter that when Officer Arnold was chasing you and Santos from the service station that he, Arnold, used vulgar language or curse words with you and Santos?

DAVID. What do you mean chasing us?

BURLESON. I mean at the time of the robbery, before they arrested you? Did he chase you?

DAVID. Nobody was chasing us.

BURLESON. And using vulgar language?

DAVID. No, sir.

BURLESON. Now, did you ever tell anyone that he used vulgar language with you and Santos as you were leaving the service station earlier that night?

DAVID. We weren't at the filling station.

BURLESON. You were not there?

DAVID. No, sir

MULDER. Objection. The defense is intimidating the witness.

BURLESON. Now, when you were at the gas station was Arnold the first one to say that there was a third suspect with the two of you when you burglarized the service station?

DAVID. It wasn't us.

BURLESON. I understand what you're saying, but was it Arnold who said there was a third person with you and Santos when you burglarized the service station?

DAVID. Yes.

BURLESON. It wasn't Cain who said that?

DAVID. No.

BURLESON. When Officer Arnold said something about the third person, did you say anything?

DAVID. No.

BURLESON. Did Santos say anything?

DAVID. Yes.

BURLESON. What did Santos say?

DAVID. He said that we weren't the fellows that did it.

BURLESON. What happened after Santos said there wasn't any third person?

DAVID. Cain took out a gun and pointed it at my brother's head.

(The scene freezes. Lights, time and space change.)

XXI. BURLESON'S REASONS

MULDER. Are you tired?

BURLESON. A little bit.

MULDER. Are you going to go?

BURLESON. I don't know.

MULDER. Come on.

BURLESON. Maybe.

MULDER. They're going to have everything.

BURLESON. Are you serious?

MULDER. Everything.

BURLESON. Hey...cool it, will you?

MULDER. What?

BURLESON. In there.

MULDER. You cool it, too.

BURLESON. What a soap opera!

MULDER. *Qué pasó?* What happened?

RUBEN. *(Entering.) No pasó,* he didn't pass. *Se quedó en Juárez.* He got stuck in Juárez. *(They both laugh.)*

BURLESON. I don't get it.

RUBEN. *(To Burleson.)* Do you like your line of work?

BURLESON. I love it.

MULDER. I couldn't do what you do.

BURLESON. But we do the same thing.

MULDER. No, you represent all kinds of people.

BURLESON. And you'll try anyone they put in front of you.

RUBEN. You have no regrets, Burleson?

BURLESON. No. I enjoy it.

RUBEN. And your conscience?

BURLESON. My what? I don't think about it.

RUBEN. Do you ever worry about making a mistake?

BURLESON. You have to go for it even if you make mistakes. But if you make a mistake, it can always be corrected.

RUBEN. Those errors can never be corrected.

BURLESON. Of course they can.

RUBEN. Do you think about justice in court?

BURLESON. Justice doesn't exist, not in court, not on the street.

MULDER. Oh, really? What about the law?

BURLESON. Law and justice are not the same. One thing is to be just, the other is legality. At least, that's the way it is in our day and age. I fear it will always be that way. Justice is a concept that comes from above. We're flesh and blood, living down below. I'm only a mortal like everyone else. But I try to find a halfway point. We're both looking to compromise, aren't we, Mulder?

RUBEN. But don't you think about the law?

BURLESON. The law is the dark shadow of justice.

MULDER. But the law exists. There are laws everywhere.

BURLESON. But they're not equal. They change from state to state. We lawyers know that the law is but a shadow of justice, and that's as close as we can get.

RUBEN. Why are you so hard on David? David sees Santos' corpse every time someone mentions him on the witness stand.

BURLESON. I see him also.

MULDER. Only his photograph.

RUBEN. How can you sleep in peace?

BURLESON. Because I'm doing my job. I have to do everything in my power to free the accused, my client.

MULDER. Almost all your clients are guilty.

BURLESON. That's why we have defense attorneys. To defend the ones who may be unjustly accused. Or doesn't the suspect have that right?

MULDER. But thanks to you the guilty go free.

BURLESON. I only do my job. That's why they pay me.

RUBEN. How can you be on Cain's side?

BURLESON. As a defense attorney, it's not my job to know the soul of the accused. I'm a lawyer, not a psychiatrist.

RUBEN. But it's your job to know the person.

BURLESON. Look, no one knows what really happened.

MULDER. If only we could look into Cain's soul.

BURLESON. Fortunately, my job is a lot simpler. All I have to do is prove it was an accident.

RUBEN. You won't be able to. Mulder won't let you. Right, Mulder? You are going to find the man guilty, aren't you?

MULDER. Well, the jury will do that. I only help them make the decision.

BURLESON. I'll help the jury...find Cain innocent.

RUBEN. But where is justice?

BURLESON. That's God's will.

XXII. BESSIE WAITS/CAIN'S NIGHTS

CAIN. It's nightfall.

BESSIE. All my days are the same.

CAIN. I'm in a dark street in the Mexican part of town.

BESSIE. I walk alone in the corridors of jail.

CAIN. It feels like someone is watching me, but I don't see him, the streets are deserted.

BESSIE. *(Holding a knife.)* I stole this from the kitchen.

CAIN. Suddenly they crawl out of the corners, the sewers.

BESSIE. I wait for him to come through the door.

CAIN. Like rats, like cockroaches.

BESSIE. I recognize him right away.

CAIN. It's them!

BESSIE. I've seen his picture in the newspapers.

CAIN. I'm afraid, very much afraid!

BESSIE. They sent him to this prison.

CAIN. They're crawling out from everywhere.

BESSIE. He's in the men's section of the prison, we run into each other...

CAIN. Black eyes glare at me with hatred.

BESSIE. In a corridor...

CAIN. They're getting closer...

BESSIE. At the entrance to the chapel...

CAIN. They are trying to trap me.

BESSIE. In the courtyard, one Sunday.

CAIN. I aim at them and fire.

BESSIE. I get close to him without his knowing.

CAIN. It doesn't stop them.

BESSIE. He doesn't know me.

CAIN. They burn, walking with their clothes on fire.

BESSIE. Rage burns inside me.

CAIN. Some fall at my feet wrapped in flames, but others appear behind them.

BESSIE. He doesn't see me take the knife out.

CAIN. They keep coming towards me.

BESSIE. Tell me the truth, I say. "I'm telling the truth," he says.

CAIN. Die, you bastards, die!

BESSIE. I'll slash his throat from ear to ear.

CAIN. There are hundreds, thousands, and I'm running out of fire.

BESSIE. I sink the knife into his heart. *(Cain cries out.)* One, two, three, seven times until I can't no more.

CAIN. My wife wakes me up. I can't get back to sleep.

BESSIE. His blood flows down the prison halls.

CAIN. And I stay awake all night thinking.

BESSIE. Then...

CAIN. Yes.

BESSIE. Then.

CAIN. Yes..

BESSIE. Then.

CAIN. Yes.

BESSIE. Santos will rest.

CAIN. We have to exterminate them.

XXIII. THE WAY IT REALLY HAPPENED

MULDER. David, could you put that chair the way it was that night, as though you were sitting in the back seat of the squad car? *(David places the chair as though he were in the squad car.)* Very well, where was Darrell Cain?

DAVID. Next to me.

MULDER. Was he sitting right there? Here?

DAVID. Yes, sir.

MULDER. Now, do you remember in which hand he had the revolver?

DAVID. In the right hand.

MULDER. The hand closest to you!

DAVID. Yes, sir.

MULDER. What did he do with the gun after he took it out of the holster?

DAVID. He pointed it at my brother's head.

MULDER. Before that, did you see him do anything with the revolver?

DAVID. Yes, sir.

MULDER. What did he do?

DAVID. He emptied the gun.

MULDER. Like this? *(Emptying the gun.)*

DAVID. Yes.

MULDER. What did he do then.

DAVID. He rolled it.

MULDER. Show me how he rolled it. *(David demonstrates.)* He twirled it like this!

DAVID. Yes, sir.

MULDER. How was he holding the gun? *(Pointing upwards.)* Like this?

DAVID. No.

MULDER. *(Pointing downwards.)* Like this?

DAVID. Yes.

MULDER. Can you tell us if the gun was loaded, if there were bullets in the cylinder or was it empty? Was the gun loaded at that moment?

DAVID. Yes, sir.

MULDER. Did you see the bullets?

DAVID. Yes.

MULDER. You didn't see empty chambers like right now?

DAVID. No, sir.

MULDER. What did Cain do after he rolled the cylinder?

DAVID. He closed it shut.

MULDER. Did you see him take any bullets out of the cylinder?

DAVID. No, sir.

MULDER. Are you sure?

DAVID. Yes.

MULDER. You were looking at the gun?

DAVID. Yes, sir.

MULDER. All right. Where was he pointing? Put my arm in the position he held the gun. Just move my arm. Point it the same way he did.

DAVID. Like this.

MULDER. Like this? Right? He was pointing...

DAVID. At Santos' head.

MULDER. Did Officer Cain say something to your brother at that moment?

DAVID. Yes, sir.

MULDER. He asked your brother if he was there when they robbed the gas station?

DAVID. If we were both there.

MULDER. What did your brother say to him?

DAVID. That we weren't there.

MULDER. Did you see Cain pull the trigger?

DAVID. Yes, sir.

MULDER. Did you hear the revolver "click?"

DAVID. Yes, sir.

MULDER. Do you remember what Cain said to your brother at that moment?

DAVID. To tell the truth.

MULDER. What did he do, David?

DAVID. He fired the gun.

MULDER. Can you show the jurors about how far he held this gun from your brother's head?

DAVID. About like this.

MULDER. Like this, right in front of your eyes?

DAVID. Yes, sir.

MULDER. Were Santos' hands still handcuffed behind his back?

DAVID. Yes, sir.

MULDER. Had he made any attempt to get out of the squad car or anything else?

DAVID. No, sir.

MULDER. All Santos did was deny he was involved in any burglary?

DAVID. Yes, sir.

MULDER. What did Cain do with the gun after he had shot Santos?

DAVID. He got out of the squad car.

MULDER. How soon did he get out of the car after he actually fired the shot that hit Santos?

DAVID. One or two seconds.

MULDER. One or two seconds. Real fast.

DAVID. Yes, sir.

MULDER. After Cain got out of the patrol car, did he have the revolver in his hand?

DAVID. Yes, sir.

MULDER. You saw the revolver in his hand?

DAVID. Yes, I was watching him because I was afraid he would shoot me.

MULDER. Were your hands still handcuffed behind you?

DAVID. Yes, sir.

MULDER. Did you get any blood on you?

DAVID. Yes.

MULDER. Did they leave you in that car with Santos?

DAVID. Yes, sir.

MULDER. Did they put you in another squad car?

DAVID. Yes.

MULDER. Hands still handcuffed behind you?

DAVID. Yes, sir.

MULDER. They locked you up?

DAVID. Yes.

MULDER. You were questioned?

DAVID. Yes.

MULDER. Did you tell them what had happened?

DAVID. Yes.

MULDER. Were you crying?

DAVID. Yes.

MULDER. All right. *(Pulling out a photograph.)* Who is this in the photograph?

DAVID. My brother.

XXIV. CONCLUSIONS

RUBEN. Why wasn't Roy Arnold tried?

MULDER. He didn't kill Santos.

RUBEN. But he fired at the suspect and didn't write it down in his report. He arrested them without proper cause. He didn't take them to the police station, but to the scene of the crime, whereupon Cain killed Santos.

MULDER. They punished Arnold; they fired him from the police force.

BURLESON. I hope the jury is fair and finds Cain not guilty.

RUBEN. Everything points to Cain's guilt. None of the prints found on the coke machine or the windows of the gas station belonged to Santos or David.

BURLESON. But when they arrested Santos and David, their clothes were sweaty, because they had run home from the gasoline station.

RUBEN. For God sake, it was summer and they didn't have air conditioning in their house.

BURLESON. They had a record of having committed burglaries.

RUBEN. Petty larceny, of no importance.

BURLESON. But they were robberies.

RUBEN. Kid's stuff.

BURLESON. Juvenile delinquents.

RUBEN. Kids without a father, their mother in jail.

BURLESON. See, they'd done this before, bad seeds.

RUBEN. And what about Cain? Two years ago he fired at a nine-year-old
black boy. Then, he and another officer tried to shoot a pair of Latinos in
the back of an empty lot. And he wasn't tried. *(To Mulder.)* Why didn't
you bring this out in the trial, Mulder?

MULDER. Because it's Santos' case, not the others.

RUBEN. O.K.! O.K.! Suppose they did do it, suppose they did break into the
gas station and steal nine dollars and a damned Coca-Cola. Don't we live
in a civilized country? Don't they have the right to due process? Who
gave him the right to shoot Santos with a dum-dum bullet? Where's their
fucking civil rights?

BURLESON. It was an accident.

RUBEN. No, it wasn't an accident that killed Santos, it wasn't the bullet from
Cain's revolver; it was fucking racism.

BURLESON. It was a terrible and lamentable accident.

RUBEN. Accident bullshit! For nine dollars and a fucking Coca-Cola...

XXV. THE VERDICT

POLICEMAN. The jury has found Officer Darrell Cain guilty of murder with
malice for the death of Santos Rodríguez. This court fines the defendant
Darrell Cain twenty dollars in court costs and sentences him to prison for
five years, sentence to be served in the Huntsville penitentiary.

XXVI. CAIN'S QUERY

CAIN. Why me? I'm a good cop. Punctual, responsible, decent. I love my
wife and kids. We go to church every Sunday. I harm no one. I obey my
superiors. I do my job. I respect the uniform I wear. What do they want
from me? I am a servant of law and order. They issue me a gun to keep
the peace. They issue me a uniform that I wear with pride. I am a
guardian of the State. I watch over the citizens. It's my duty; I do it with
pleasure. Why do they accuse me? I believe in the Dallas Police

Department. I believe in the United States of America. I swore to defend my country. God is on our side. What did I do wrong? This is a free country, the best country. I don't know what happened, it was an impulse, something made me do it. Who pushed my hand? Who programmed my mind? I don't know. But I'm not an evil person, I swear to God!

THE END